HELP! I'M BEING BULLIED

Dr Emily Lovegrove

Published by Accent Press Ltd – 2006
ISBN 1905170343

Printed and bound in the UK by
Cox & Wyman, Reading

Cover Design by Anna Torborg

The publisher acknowledges the financial support
of the Welsh Books Council

This book is dedicated to the memory of *my* Mum
and Dad – Shirley and Laurie.

ACKNOWLEDGEMENTS:

My huge thanks to ALL those wonderful teenagers who gave me their time, their energy and their knowledge – in telling me about their lives and in helping me to develop these anti-bullying strategies. You were all stars.

And thank you too to the families who let me describe what happened to them. Even though you all coped brilliantly and everyone will be impressed with you, I've changed all your names so that there is absolutely no risk of embarrassment!

More huge thanks also to husband Chris who designed the strategy symbols for me as well as my friends Cathy Salah, Bea Hope, Jo Sheff, Sue Potts, Susan Edwards – and Tammy (15) plus Guto (11) – who read various early drafts of this book! My thanks also to Cassey Aspinall at Seattle Children's Hospital.

Thank you too to Hazel and Bob Cushion of Accent Press for all your encouragement and enthusiasm.

CONTENTS

Introduction	Adults	1
Chapter 1	Adults – Is it bullying? Stop & think!	5
Chapter 1	Kids – Is it bullying? Stop & think!	21
Chapter 2	Adults – Self-Motto	38
Chapter 2	Kids – Self-Motto	50
Chapter 3	Adults – Other-Motto	64
Chapter 3	Kids – Other-Motto	78
Chapter 4	Adults – Distraction, Humour, Friends	91
Chapter 4	Kids – Distraction, Humour, Friends	105
Chapter 5	Adults – Appearance, Flattery, Reward	115
Chapter 5	Kids – Appearance, Flattery, Reward	129
Chapter 6	Adults – Using ALL the strategies!	138
Chapter 6	Kids – Using ALL the strategies!	153

INTRODUCTION

Help! My child is being bullied and I'm desperate...

You've seen the headlines ('*Distraught parents of suicide victim blame school for not addressing bullying problem*'), you've felt the fear. And now you are stuck in that place where your child tells you that if you get out there and do something they risk further bullying.

But if you do nothing... You both know they *still* risk further bullying. Being bullied at school is HORRIBLE. And being the parent of a child who is being bullied is also *horrible.* And while we're on the subject, being a teacher or other professional working with children who are being bullied is not much fun either. Most adults want to help. Very few know *how.*

Remember this feeling of hopelessness and helplessness... Why? Because by the end of this book it's going to be a distant memory. You are going to have TEN proven, successful strategies that will change the way you deal with aggression. And because you are your child's role model they will copy you. So then THEY will have ten proven, successful ways of dealing with anything nasty that life chucks their way too!

The very first thing is – you're going to have to stop struggling and relax. Tension makes *everything* worse. Turn off the mobile, find somewhere nice to sit down and get reading. The sooner you do this the sooner you're going to feel back in control as a family. What could you possibly be waiting for?

People have been struggling with this problem of bullying for years – how can you say it's this easy?
I didn't say it was easy! You're going to have to:
- Read the book
- Look at how you yourself cope with bullying
- Do some exercises that raise your awareness
- Learn some strategies and
- Work out how you can put them into practice

And on top of that you're going to have to help your child do the same thing!

Excuse me, but who exactly are you?
I'm married to a schoolteacher and I'm mum to three adult kids. I'm grandmother to four gorgeous grandchildren and over the years I've had various cats, rabbits, guinea pigs and hens. Even, for one week, a dog (it's a long story)… Er… you don't mean that sort of information, do you? You mean what are my qualifications for offering you advice on coping with bullying! Right! I'm a psychologist. Psychologists use the knowledge we currently have – based on scientific evidence about how our brains work and how we generally behave – to achieve the most helpful

2

solution to people problems. Me? I spent years researching the topic of children, their appearance and bullying as well as lecturing in a university. Based on that research I then worked with teenagers to develop and test the anti-bullying strategies they found the most useful. Now I spend my time as a consultant, helping schools all over the UK and hospitals (such as Great Ormond Street UK, and Seattle Children's USA), as well as families, put those strategies that the teenagers and I developed to practical use.

Why are there two parts to this book?

This book is designed to be helpful for adults and for kids. So each topic is dealt with first in a chapter for you, and then in one for them. The adult chapters give you the technical stuff (*why* each strategy is important). The alternate chapters are then aimed at your child. If you have younger children you can work through their chapters together. Older kids may well be able – or prefer – to work at theirs by themselves. The important thing is that you will understand what they're trying to achieve – and why. And equally importantly, they will know that you understand the techniques they're learning and that you're there to help them.

And that's what this book is about – helping you work together to raise self-esteem and overcome bullying! What's more, hard though this may seem when things are tough, it's jolly well going to be FUN!

ADULTS – CHAPTER 1

BULLYING? STOP&THINK!

In this chapter I'm going to give you answers to the questions that parents always ask me about bullying. I'll also tell you what kids say about it. Best of all, *by the end of this chapter you will already have the first TWO vital strategies that you need to help you sort out bullying!*

Why have I got to do this? Why aren't schools dealing with it?

They DO try to deal with it. Every school has to have an anti-bullying policy. And you are entitled (and usually encouraged) to read it. This document will probably say something along the lines of:

* *This school does not tolerate bullying!*

In theory this sounds like a good aim to have but it's a bit woolly and you know it isn't working because your child IS being bullied!

Then the school policy will probably *define* bullying and say something like:

* *Bullying can be physical.*

This means anything you can see like hitting, punching, kicking, spitting, stealing, or unpleasant phone texts. Schools deal pretty well with this kind of bullying. After all, there is usually proof in the form of bruises, lost possessions or nasty mobile messages. Kids say that despite all the publicity it gets there is a relatively small amount of physical bullying.

- *Bullying can be psychological.*

This means anything you can't really pin down like excluding kids from groups, calling names, spreading rumours or giving nasty looks. Schools tend *not* to deal well with this kind of bullying. They find it difficult for the same reasons that everyone else finds it difficult. Some of them don't regard this kind of bullying as real bullying and call it teasing and assume this isn't so bad. Most don't *know* how to deal with it. And an awful lot of teachers can't deal with it when it happens to them either. Kids say there is a *huge* amount of psychological bullying. This is a MAJOR problem because it means that *the bulk of bullying is never tackled*. Not only that, *psychological bullying that isn't dealt with successfully often leads to physical bullying…*

- *To count as physical or psychological bullying, it must be repeated and intentional.*

The theory behind this is that teachers will not have to spend the entire school day sorting out every knock, unfortunate glance and tripping up over a casually placed satchel! BUT – what happens about the child who is clever enough to realise that they can technically get away with one unseen, violent threat or vicious comment? They'll quickly find their opportunity to intimidate a whole class on the first day of the new school year! And how do you cope with the child who is insensitive and claims they 'did not mean to bully'?

All you *can* do is work on your own children's emotional and social skills in case school cannot (or even will not) help. Armed with the whole raft of anti-bullying strategies you're going to have, you and they are going to feel hugely more powerful at sorting this kind of stuff out for yourselves!

People give us all sorts of confusing advice...

Below is a list of the kind of things people say about bullying. Take some time to look at them and think about what they're saying:

• *Being bullied makes you a stronger person.*

There are *some* people who have triumphed over bullying eventually and let us know that they didn't let it stop them doing what they wanted. But for the majority of people this is not true. Their self-esteem goes down, they stop believing the world is a wonderful place. They don't feel any stronger.

• *Bullies are stupid people who hit you for no reason.*

Bullies raise their self-esteem by putting others down. In order to do this they need to be aware of what will humiliate others. To do this, bullies have to have quite well developed social skills. The more intelligent they are, the more skilled the bullying.

- *Just ignore them and they'll stop.*

They WON'T! Bullies require your attention. Ignoring them means they have to try a whole lot harder to get it!

- *Invite bullies to tea – then you'll be friends.*

Great. Now not only do they make your child's life miserable at school, they also feel that they have you on their side! By all means arrange outings together that foster friendships, just don't do it in your own home where your child feels safe.

- *It was only a bit of fun – can't you take a joke?*

Children (and adults too) often laugh when they're embarrassed. It doesn't mean they found the physical or psychological bullying genuinely funny.

- *Bullies have no friends.*

They do. Quite often they are your child's friends too. There will be children who genuinely like them and there will be children who are superficially friendly with them to avoid being bullied next. Either way they are rarely friendless.

- *They were asking for it.*

This is a difficult one. Logically we feel that no one asks to be bullied. In practice though there are children who are so desperate for attention they DO seem to invite bullying by provoking other children until they get a reaction.

So what can we do about bullying?

Suppose your child is being bullied. Is it fair that this poor child, who has done nothing wrong, should have

8

to learn new ways of coping and change their behaviour? Lots of parents feel this implies I'm suggesting that their child is at fault. They argue that the *bully* is the one who needs to change. Let's be very clear here. This is not a book that is going to say that all bullies are wicked, evil demons (the flogging-and-hanging's-too-good-for-them approach!). Nor will it say (despite the awful distress they endure) that their victims are wonderful, gentle souls who wouldn't harm a fly. *All* of us are capable of causing distress and being bullies given the right circumstances.

Are you saying I'm a bully?

I'm only saying that humans are very sociable creatures. We constantly look at others and compare ourselves to see where we fit in. And if we feel that we are always being put down or not achieving as much as others, one of the ways we *can* feel better about ourselves is to make someone else feel a little worse. We even justify this to ourselves by thinking of it as 'evening things up'!

I'll give you an example. Suppose one kid in your child's class always does well at maths. Fair enough, but this kid's mum goes on and *on* about it. "Eloise's teacher can hardly keep up with her you know. She thinks Eloise is one of the brightest children she has *ever* taught!" Can you honestly swear, hand on heart, that you would never wish to subtly point out to Eloise's mum how much better your child is than hers at PE / spelling, and how easy *your* child finds those things? Me neither! But we also have to take on board that if our kids watch, or hear about adults scoring points this way, they'll soon learn to copy!

The big point here is that once your child is introduced to any social group, they will need to fit in. And you will need to help them to do that. Because once they are with this group of other children, it is those other children who will protect or harm them. *You will not be there…*

You said you had done research into this…
What did you do?
The first part of my research was with about 1,000 children and teenagers, looking at what they see as bullying – and what they want to happen if they're being bullied. The second part was helping them to sort out what skills they needed to do that. And then, because I had to be able to demonstrate that what I said actually works, I did lots of testing on kids to show that learning and using those skills was successful. The final bit of the research was to get my work published in an academic journal so that the information was there for anyone to read and use.

One of my main findings was that kids see bullying as strongly related to their appearance.

I'm going to stop reading right here if you're going to suggest that we spend our money on designer labels for our kids!
Trust me, I'm *not* going to do that. I'm just sharing

with you the finding that when I did my research with all those children and teenagers, there was huge concern over the way they look. And if you remember that over 80% of communication is non-verbal (which means we all pick up 80% of our clues about people just from the way they appear to us – their clothes, their body language, their tone of voice) you can see *why* children and teenagers instinctively feel that way!

What else did all these children and teenagers say then?
1. 3 out of 4 young teenagers said that the thing they are most afraid of at school is teasing or bullying about their appearance –"*I spend my whole life trying to look prettier and thinner so that no one can call me fat.*" (Eleanor, aged 16)
2. Nearly half of them said that they feel very uncomfortable around people who look different from them – "*Of course we don't like them [a group of Goths], they look weird.*" (Ryan, aged 18)
3. 1 in 3 said they don't want to speak up in class because they feel bad about they way they look – "*You don't want people to laugh at you when you don't look right, so you don't put your hand up to answer the teacher.*" (Lottie, aged 14)
4. 1 in 5 said that their families are very critical of their appearance – "*I have hardly any friends and my mum says that's down to how I look. She calls me a freak.*" (Andrew, aged 17)
5. 1 in 5 of all the 15 year-olds I talked to said that

some days they truant from school because of the way they look – *"If you look bad you get bullied so you just stay home."* (Aaron, aged 15)

So the way they look is *really* important to them and they know that somehow this is definitely linked to getting teased and bullied. And we can see from these kids' comments that their fear of teasing and bullying doesn't just affect their confidence and happiness, it has a negative affect on their schoolwork too!

If we want to help them to sort out bullying, we have to take this on board.

Of course, you and I know that what really matters is their personality and that WE don't judge people by the way they look. We are not that shallow! *Or are we?* Have a look at the next few statements and tell me what you think about them…

- *Blondes have more fun!*

I'm currently blonde so I'll say yes to that one! But is there any scientific research to suggest I'm right? Well there IS research that says the human brain notices light things faster than dark things so the chances are that blondes get noticed quicker. And that could be an advantage in certain circumstances – like a dimly lit pub! Of course, there is *also* research that shows that people think that brunettes are cleverer. That might explain why we have those daft stereotypes of blonde bimbos and dark-haired, straight-laced career women.

12

You've lost me there already... what do you mean when you say a stereotype?

It's when you lump a whole lot of people together because they are similar in some way. You might mean to be complimentary (such as 'Afro-Caribbeans have a great sense of rhythm' or 'Asians are good at maths') or you could intend to be offensive (such as 'Teenagers are thugs' or 'Old people smell'). Stereotypes are nearly always unhelpful because using them means we've stopped looking at people as individuals. Not all blondes are dizzy and not all brunettes are clever! But back to our quiz...

- *Tall, good-looking men / slim, attractive women earn up to 10% more than their less attractive colleagues.*

Could that possibly be true? You suspect it might be, don't you? But it's worse than that – they earn up to **15%** more! And it's not all good news for them – another piece of research showed that good-looking men who are convicted of crimes get longer sentences on average because judges think 'their looks already give them advantages over those who are less attractive'! It's also scary to realise that most juries decide whether someone is guilty or not within about 7 seconds of first seeing them.

- *That which is beautiful is good.*

Are beautiful people always good? Well of course they aren't! But... if they aren't, why can you always spot the baddie in films (think Freddie Kruger)? And think of all those fairy stories we were brought up on that have the hero as handsome and the heroine as beautiful. Let alone those plain but useful women who suddenly whip off their glasses and let their hair down to the shocked and delighted cry of "Why, you're beautiful, Miss Jones, I'd never realised!" It might make you spit, but you'll recognise it as being a tried and tested film cliché. This means that although we might *say* appearance doesn't matter, in reality, whether we like it or not, we certainly *behave* as if it does.

- *Beautiful people are more popular!*

This is a toughie. We rather suspect this one might be true. But the good news here is that it isn't necessarily so. The answer is that *it is those people who have the best social and emotional skills who are the most popular*. The difficulty is, if you were faced with the decision to *either* have plastic surgery, a style consultant and a personal trainer *or* develop the social and emotional skills that make you popular – which would you choose? Whatever your answer was to this, chances are your child would copy you and have the same response because *you* are their role model. Unless you *really* want them to rely solely on surgery for their sense of worth, helping them acquire those skills would be a very smart move.

Fascinating! But what else did kids tell you about bullying?
1. *Kids don't just want bullying to stop, they also want to be liked by other kids – even by the bullies (who are sometimes their friends).*

This is VERY important because it means that they

(and we) have to be much more careful about sorting the bullying out. Human beings are hardwired to work best in groups. Kids very sensibly know that to be isolated at school is a very scary position indeed.

2. *Kids want to know how to sort out minor bullying for themselves rather than have to rely on adults.*

After all, how would YOU feel if every time you were upset you had to ask somebody else to sort it for you? It's not very empowering, is it?

3. *The ways of coping that kids use most are hitting and shouting back or running away and truanting.*

Even though they know that these strategies are not popular with teachers or parents. And also even though they often don't work! Most kids see these as their only options.

4. *Kids also say that when they ask adults what else they could do, they are told to either ignore bullies or tell an adult.*

Children in their hundreds have told me that these strategies on their own, with nothing to back them up, are hardly ever successful.

5. *What kids particularly wanted was a range of skills that would give them choices in how to deal positively with awkward situations.*

So that's what I gave them. Ten different, successful strategies (ways of coping) that help them to be more popular in school and empower them to deal with bullying in a positive way.

15

How?

What I did was to ask various groups of teenagers to look at the anti-bullying strategies that were only available to children and adults who were picked on because of their severe disfigurements. I asked my groups of teenagers to help me adapt those strategies and develop some new ones for all children and young people to use. Teenagers may have a reputation for being sulky and difficult, but every one of the ones I asked to help was fantastic. They gave up hours of their time to look at books and films and help sort out which strategies they really needed to help them cope. And then they practised using those adapted and new strategies to see which ones really worked. Eventually they even helped me to write up the successful strategies as a series of school lessons! All absolute stars, I couldn't possibly have done it without them.

What happened next?

I went on to teach hundreds of other school children the strategies and to test them *before* I taught them and again *six months later* to see if learning them had been as helpful to them as we had all hoped.

And?

Even though all I'd worked on in the school sessions was dealing with teasing and bullying about *appearance*, 6 months after pupils had been taught these strategies (and had had time to practice them)

I found that:
1. They were *much* more confident about coping with all sorts of bullying – whether it happened to them or to someone else.
2. They had higher self-esteem – and not just about appearance but about things like schoolwork and sport.
3. Bullying was reduced by two thirds – from 59% saying they had been bullied in the last six months down to 21%.

So if the information is out there, why aren't teachers using it?

Although the government and local authorities say they want schools to address bullying, there is *still* hardly any help with it in our teacher training colleges. That's why lots of teachers will also be reading this book. They too have had that despairing feeling of how on earth can we help to sort bullying out! And not only teachers – health professionals also have patients who have problems with appearance-related bullying that undermines their ability to get well.

But why do I need to do any exercises? I can already cope for myself.

That's good news. But the truth is, most adults find it difficult to suggest the best solutions because *they're* not sure how to deal with bullying in a positive way either. Tell me, what do you suggest when someone is making your child feel insignificant and wretched? In exasperation do you suggest they shout back, *"You are fatter / more stupid than me"*? Or even, *"Just hit them – hard!"* Although you know that isn't the way you really want your kids to learn to behave, like a bully, you feel desperate because you can't think of anything else! Or maybe this worked for *you* when you were at school. The trouble is, shouting and hitting back could just as easily make things even worse and then everything will be that much harder to sort out...

So what exercises do you want me to do?
In this instance they are exactly the same ones that I'm asking your child to do in the next chapter! They'll like it if you do this too because it will reinforce the message that even though they don't want you to interfere at school, you're still willing to do something to help them.

OK, you've convinced me! How do I use this book?
You star! Here goes...
- Since it's really hard to teach children something we haven't done for ourselves (think new maths!), for each strategy there is a chapter for you with the information you need to know *before you do the exercises with your child*.
- Younger children have a much shorter concentration span than older ones. You need to decide on how long you can work together on an

18

exercise before a) They lose interest or b) You lose the will to live! *Set aside an agreed amount of time, decide on a small reward each for doing the exercises, do them, and then reward yourselves!*

- If children are in the middle of a bullying situation, working straight away on their own situation can feel very threatening for both of you. *So each strategy will have a general, non-personal example to work through first.* Most children will be able to apply this example to their own situation without much further guidance. But if not, remember to go *SLOWLY* – the last thing we want is for them to feel they're now failing to understand how to sort out their problems! Trust me – they *WILL* get there, it just might not be in quite the way you expected!

- This is a feel-good book! It will finally give you the strategies you need to help your child cope for themselves with threats, teasing, being left out, nasty looks, and feeling that school years are possibly the worst of their whole life!

Hey! You said I'd learn two strategies in this chapter! Which ones am I supposed to have learned?

You now have TWO fundamentally important strategies to help you and your child sort out any bullying.

1. BULLYING? This is the strategy that asks us to check whether bullying has actually occurred. Whatever the school anti-bullying policy says, it's not 'just teasing' if your child finds it hurtful – and

people don't have to be *deliberately* nasty to cause them pain. If they feel someone has humiliated them, or made them feel small, it is bullying.

It's really important to know that it IS bullying if you feel it is. Instead of wasting energy justifying yourself to people who think it really isn't, you can now use your energy to help your child use positive strategies to feel better about themselves.

2. STOP&THINK! This is the strategy that recognises that how you sort it out depends on what you want to happen eventually. So if your child wants to stay friends with someone, even though that child has been mean to them, this will make a big difference to how they choose to sort it out.

This strategy is another really good one because it makes us consider the OUTCOME before we set off a chain of events in helping children towards a solution that might not, in the end, actually suit them!

What's in it for us?

When your children grow up they may forget / not care that you gave them new bikes / piano lessons. But they will NEVER STOP BEING GRATEFUL to you for helping them to cope successfully with bullying!

Kids - Chapter I

Hi! If you picked up this book for yourself – or if some kind person gave it to you – I guess you may have a problem with being bullied…

The BAD news is that right now you probably feel pretty fed-up about it. You feel you're at the mercy of some horrible other kid or grown-up who makes your life miserable. You probably feel there's not much you can do about it. The WORST thing about being bullied is that you feel powerless.

The GOOD news is that by the end of this book you will feel MUCH BETTER! And if you're clever enough to want to sort out your bullying problems, you are behaving in a very mature way so I'm going to treat you like, say, a university student. I'm going to offer you TEN anti-bullying strategies (this means ten ways of coping with bullying) and in this chapter we are going to learn the first TWO!

But first off I'd better introduce myself. I'm called Emily – I'm sorry that I don't know your name but it will *feel* like we're friends by the end of the book! I used to work in a university as a researcher. This means that the university paid me to look at people's problems and see if I could come up with some solutions. And the thing I looked at in particular was schools and bullying. And, the most important part, how YOU can use what I found out to help you STOP the bullying...

One of the really great things about my job is that I get to spend a huge amount of time listening to people your age talk about stuff that is important to them. For instance, do you know what three quarters of pupils said are the two very WORST things about school?

1. They get teased or bullied.
2. They are *afraid* of getting teased and bullied.

They all said that they'd had classes at school on what bullying *is* but it still felt like grown-ups thought that things like name-calling and giving bad looks were only *teasing* and not so bad. They also said that to them teasing was *just as bad* as being hit or shouted at. They felt that perhaps grown-ups like to say teasing isn't so bad because they feel they can't do anything about it... So the kids I worked with came up with a slightly different way of saying what bullying is. They agreed it could be ANYTHING that makes you feel small or stupid. If you *feel* as if you've been bullied, then you probably *have* been bullied.

We also agreed that there are lots of ideas out there that make it harder to know what to think. Have a look at the statements below and see if you think they are true or false…

It's only bullying if someone hits you.
Definitely, definitely not true! Somebody asked loads of grown-ups if they'd been bullied at school and what upset them most. It wasn't the ones who'd been hit that were still upset. It was the ones who'd had nasty things said about them. Why do YOU think this might be so? I'd agree with you if you thought it was something to do with them still feeling small or humiliated inside even now they've grown up.

Being bullied makes you a stronger person.
If you learn to tackle bullies successfully this is definitely true. If you do not learn how to tackle bullies successfully, it is definitely false. The trouble is, you get the odd person for whom this is true. They had a horrible time at school and when they left they were determined not to let it get them down and now they're managing director of their own firm. But then you start thinking, "What's wrong with me, because being picked on makes just me feel weaker, not stronger". Being picked on makes most of us feel weaker.

Bullies are stupid people who hit you for no reason.
Not true! Bullies are often very clever people who can pick up on our secret feelings about ourselves. They hit you because they look at you and think they can get away with it. Hitting out makes them feel more powerful and in control. This is how they feel better about themselves. Remembering this is good because it helps you to see that bullying is quite complicated. Knowing this means that you won't be tempted to look for easy answers – you will understand that you need a whole range of solutions to be able to cope successfully.

Just hit them back and they'll stop.
Not if they are bigger / hit harder / have a very big brother who hits harder! But I can see how sometimes this solution might seem really tempting. I need to explain something really important to you here... We do things because we get rewarded for doing them. For instance, you might clean your teeth because you like the feeling of shiny teeth. Or you might do it because your mum will be cross if you don't. But the reason you do it is for that reward (feeling clean or pleasing your mum). It's the same with hitting back. If you do it and it stops the bullying, that feels like a reward. And if other kids give you respect for hitting the bully that's another reward! You might well now feel that hitting back is the answer. For now, I need you to remember that even though hitting back might stop the bullying and other kids might respect you

more, hitting back is not respectful in the long term. If you keep working at this, in this book we'll learn MUCH more useful ways to make you even more popular!

Just ignore bullies and they'll stop.
It is very hard indeed to ignore someone who is trying hard to make you feel small. And this is exactly why bullies pick on you. They can see that you have fewer ways of coping with bullying than they do! Not only that, they bully you to get a reaction. If you don't react, they often try a lot harder to upset you so that they can get that kick out of making you look small.

Invite bullies to tea with you – then you'll be friends.
Yup! I'm sure you want someone who is making your life miserable at school to come to your house, have your mum be nice to them, and see all your toys (not)! But sometimes it can work if you could find something that you both like doing and can do that together (like join a swimming club).

It was only a bit of fun – can't you even take a joke?
Well funnily enough NO! Not when the joke is just to make you look stupid you can't! Trouble is, sometimes we DO laugh back but that's because we are embarrassed. It still doesn't make it funny. It just means that someone picked up on some of your real feelings about yourself and realised how to make you feel small.

Bullies have no friends.

Yes they do! Sometimes other kids stay friendly with bullies so that they don't get bullied. Sometimes other kids stay friendly with bullies because they both enjoy the same things. Sometimes other kids stay friendly with bullies because the bully is actually very nice to them. Sometimes the bully is your friend too...

Grown-ups know how to sort out bullying.

You know this one isn't true! If grown-ups know all that stuff they should be able to sort it out when YOU get bullied. Of course, in YOUR case you do have a grown-up who is trying to sort it out by going through this book with you. By the end, you will BOTH be able to sort it out! But it's worth remembering that some grown-ups have only learnt one or two ways of coping with bullies. Usually these are the people who say you should ignore bullies or tell a grown-up. And this might have worked for them. What you understand now is that only having one or two ways to sort out bullying is a bit limited! If bullies feel rewarded by being unkind, we're going to have to work hard to change that!

Our school does not have any bullying.

Not only does EVERY school have problems with bullying, lots of schools – without meaning to – ENCOURAGE bullying! For instance, if your school plays rugby, football or hockey, some teams are encouraged to intimidate (frighten) the opposing team when the match is against other schools. How is it OK to scare other kids for matches but expect the team not to do that the rest of the time? And what if the head teacher isn't the good leader we need them to be? Or your class teacher?

It doesn't hurt unless it happens to you.
Actually it does still hurt! Grown-ups who had left school a long time ago were asked about bullying when they were at school. They were still as upset about bullying that happened to other people as they were about bullying that happened to themselves. After all, if it was your friend who was bullied, and you couldn't help them, wouldn't you feel bad too? This is also what it feels like for parents when their children get bullied. They feel really helpless and upset. The brilliant thing is, once you know how to tackle bullies for yourself, you can see how to help your friends or your family when they get bullied. Great, isn't it?

They were asking for it.
This is a really difficult one. Do you remember that we talked earlier about doing things because there is some sort of reward in it for us? Well SOMETIMES people seem to encourage others to bully them because getting bad attention is better (to them) than getting no attention at all. For instance, can you think of times when you might have behaved badly at home in order to get your mum's or dad's attention? Whoops!

Bullying *stops* when you *leave* school.

We wish! Kids bully other kids because they do not feel good about themselves. Because they don't know any other way to feel better about themselves they put other kids down. And grown-ups do exactly the same. Not being bullied at school, or when you leave school, does NOT depend on if you are clever, or rich, or fantastic looking. Clever, rich and beautiful people get bullied too you know! Coping with bullying DEPENDS ON YOU! And that's why you're reading this book and learning lots of useful solutions that will help you for the rest of your life!

The kids I talked with also said what they were teased or bullied about the most. Can you guess what it was? It was people picking on THE WAY THEY LOOKED!

Does this surprise you?

Or are you thinking, *"I knew that straight away!"*

The trouble was, even though they all knew it, nobody could think of a solution to this problem that really worked… What about a make-over? After all, there are loads of TV programmes that take people who hate the way they look and make them feel great about themselves. At the end they all say how confident they feel now…

Suppose YOU were being bullied, and you got taken to a company who sorted out your hair and dressed you in amazing clothes. Do you think that would be the whole answer to your problems? Take a few minutes to think about this…

- THREE gold stars if you thought it might make you feel brilliant and that feeling brilliant might help you be more confident at dealing with the bullies.
- FIVE gold stars if you also thought 'What about later on, when no one was there to sort out my hair, and what if my parents couldn't afford endless new clothes?'
- And TEN gold stars if you went on to remember that even very beautiful, fashionable people get bullied too, so it's going to take more than a make-over!
- And just in case there are some of you whose brains are working overtime here, about TWENTY gold stars if you thought about those people who are born looking so different that even a hundred operations won't completely make them look the way they'd like to be. *And* all those who are in accidents or have illnesses that also make them look really different. A makeover is not going to do it for them either, is it?

But how would you feel if I told you that the answer to your problem has been partly solved by this group of people who look very different? The thing is, if you see someone like that, you kind of guess that they're going to get bullied about their appearance by other people. And you're right, of course, they do. Worse still, they also get stared at and people make comments about them.

What would YOU do if you thought you looked different from all your mates, you got stared at and people made comments about you? Would you:

- Stare back or shout at them?
- Look at the floor or not go out?

Yes, and that's exactly what they did too. And we understand why. But this is a big problem because if you do either of those things, people tend not to get to know you as a person. And if people don't get to know you, you don't have many friends. And now you have TWO problems instead of one... This is *particularly* difficult because most kids say that they not only want bullying to stop, they want to be popular too!

So some adults started looking at how to help these kids make friends and feel better about themselves. They came up with some anti-bullying strategies (ways of sorting out bullying) that made these kids feel a whole lot more confident about coping with bullying *and* about going out and making friends.

Which is particularly good for you. Why? Because as soon as I found out in *my* work how upset *most* kids of your age are about the way they look and being bullied, I asked lots of groups of fantastic teenagers to help me to develop those anti-bullying strategies (ways of coping with bullying) for YOU to use too.

The main problem is that we think that when people pick on the way we *look* the answer is to change that thing. The 'If someone laughs at your specs, get contact lenses' kind of solution. But does that always work? Most kids say 'No, it doesn't – bullies just look for something else about you to pick on'.

So the thing we need to do is to find what the actual link is between how we look (our appearance) and why we get bullied... This is a bit fiddly, but we'll do it in bite-sized chunks as we go through this book!

First off, we need to understand a bit about how our brains work.

And then we need to understand a bit about how our brains affect our feelings.

And lastly, we need to see how those feelings affect how we behave!

And because I'm a scientist, we'll do it as short, scientific experiments. If you quickly work your way through these experiments, by the end of the book you will not only know *what* happens and *why*, you will *understand how you can change what happens to you.*

So let's start! *It's really easy and at least no one's going to give you marks out of ten, or say you did it wrong!* I've suggested to your parents that they do this experiment too so let them have a go and be easy on them! They don't need to be marked out of ten either!

First part of Experiment number I, Part I...
Supposing I tell you that I was watching you today and I thought your day was HORRIBLE. I thought you had a DREADFUL time!

31

Could you tell me all the BAD things that happened to you?

Just think about it...

Did it rain?

Was a teacher grumpy?

Did anyone shout at you *for no reason*?

Did any of your friends ignore you at break-time?

Have you felt pretty miserable at any stage?

Did any other things happen that made you feel bad?

YES? I thought so! Poor, POOR you – you DID have a horrible day... I expect you feel awful...

Experiment number 1, Part 2...

Suppose I now tell you that I just lied to you! Whoops!

Actually when I watched you today I thought you had a GREAT day! I thought you did really BRILLIANTLY!

Just run me through all the GOOD things that happened...

Did you enjoy the sun/rain/wind at any part of the day?

Did you get something nice for one of your meals?

Did you get chosen for anything today?

Did your mum or dad give you a hug?

Were there other things that made you laugh, or even for a little time feel great?

YES? Excellent! I was right, you did have a great day! I bet you feel really good about yourself...

Well, THAT wasn't too painful as an experiment, was it?

How did it work? The answer is in understanding how your brain works. One big thing you need to realise in your quest to stop being bullied is:

Your brain is a little bit like a search engine on a computer.

What that means is – YOU are the boss. YOU decide to put into your brain the message of what you want to find:

"Bring me everything horrible that happened today!"

OR

"Bring me everything good that happened today!"

And your brain looks for all the bad or good things that it can find stored away in your memory!

Your brain *doesn't care what you ask* – it just whizzes around and answers the question that YOU set it.

What's more, the more often you ask your brain for certain answers, the quicker it gets at producing them. This is why you don't have to get your brain to think much about how you get dressed – you've done it so often your brain can just get on with instructions to your hands, legs, arms and feet without you feeling you're doing much thinking at all... Well, unless you're going to a party of course – which is a whole different ball game!

Anyway, this is just one of the brilliant things that brains do. But in this case, there is also a problem with the brain getting speedy at doing things often. Because if you always ask your brain for a list of *bad* things, you might start to think that *only* bad things happen to you. And that gets us on to the feelings part because if you think that only bad things happen to you, you will probably start to feel VERY miserable…

The flip side of this is that if you keep asking your brain to come up with a list of all the good things that happen, *without doing anything else*, you should actually start to feel better about things – *even if you are still being bullied*!

But I did say I was a scientist, so I don't want you to take my word for it without you checking it out for yourself…

YOU are now the scientist. Try this experiment and see what happens to you… I've written it out so that you can put in your answers. At the end, you can do what all scientists do – you can look at what happened and make some conclusions about what you found.

Experiment number 2, Part 1
Remember three BAD things that happened today

-
-
-

Now tell me how you FEEL once you remember the BAD things that happened. Do you feel better about yourself, or do you feel worse about yourself?

I feel… _____ about myself

Experiment number 2, Part 2

Remember three GOOD things that happened today

-
-
-

Tell me how you FEEL after you remembered the GOOD things that happened today. Do you now feel better about yourself or worse about yourself?

I feel... _____ about myself

Now tell me how you FEEL about yourself once you remember the AWFUL things that happened. Do you feel better, or do you feel worse?

I feel... _____ about myself

So how did YOU get on with the experiment?

If you were like all the other people your age who've done it:

1. You probably felt much *worse* about yourself after you remembered the *bad, horrible, nasty* things that happened. And your feelings will have made a difference to your appearance because they will have shown in your face.

2. You probably felt much *better* about yourself after you remembered the *good, nice, fantastic* things! And this will also have changed your appearance because these feelings will have shown on your face too.

IMPORTANT...
1. YOU were the one controlling what your brain remembered.
2. Because you control what you remember, YOU were the one controlling your feelings.
3. Because you can control your feelings, YOU changed how your face looks.

Interesting, isn't it?

I'm not saying that you shouldn't ever think about bad things because that would be really stupid of me. Bad things happen and sometimes we need to think about them because that helps us to get over them, or grow as human beings. But what I am suggesting is that even when bad things happen we can remember that we have the power to change how we feel about it just by being careful what we put into our brain search engines.

Brilliant! Even if you didn't realise it, you now have the first TWO strategies you need to sort out bullying!

STRATEGY NUMBER 1: BULLYING?

This is the strategy you use first of all to decide for yourself whether YOU feel you have been bullied. It doesn't matter if somebody else says, "It's only teasing!" If you feel you've been bullied – you have!

• DON'T waste any more energy on sorting this part out, you've been bullied and you are allowed to feel angry and upset.

- DO use energy to sort the bullying out in a positive way by using the other strategies you're going to learn!

STRATEGY NUMBER 2: STOP&THINK!
This strategy is the one you use to remind yourself that how you deal with being bullied depends on what you want to happen in the end. What MOST people want is the bullying to stop AND still keep or make friends. You now understand that this will mean learning some new ways of thinking.

So what about those experiments? Was learning that you might not be able to change what happens but you can change your feelings a strategy? Well, doing the experiment *wasn't* learning a particular strategy but it *was* learning a useful skill that you're going to need for the next strategy, in the next chapter!

ADULTS – CHAPTER 2

SELF-MOTTO

Technical bit...

In our heads, whatever is happening, there is a kind of internal monologue as we chat silently to ourselves throughout the day. The "Need to get those files now – Good grief what *is* she wearing – It's nearly four o'clock – Is that toothache coming on?" sort of chatter that means we are awake! What we know from clinical psychologists (the kind of psychologists who work in hospitals) is that there is a fundamental difference in this silent, internal chatter between those people who feel *unable* to cope, and those people who can cope. The ones who can't cope keep thinking only about the bad things that have happened – "Why do I always get things wrong – no one likes me or cares about me" sort of thoughts. If you asked them to sum up what sort of person they are, based on how they think about themselves, they are likely to say, "I'm useless. I expect no one really likes me."

For the sake of argument, we're going to call this

view of ourselves our 'self-motto'. People who have a negative self-motto often feel miserable, isolated and exhausted. So if your child says they feel wretched but doesn't appear to be doing anything positive about it, this is probably why. Their negative view of themselves means they can't find the energy to do anything about it. The task here is to get them to change that silent, destructive talk that's going on in their heads into something more useful. Something that will give them lots of positive energy. We did an easy version of it in the experiment number 2 in their first chapter. Learning how to make our self-motto work for us in a positive way is going to be our next strategy...

Example:

Rhiannon and David are both full-time, working parents to Laura, aged five, and Christopher, aged three. Rhiannon and David work near one another, and Laura's school has a nursery that Christopher attends. They all set off together in the car each day. Both parents get really upset that however organised they try to be, it takes very little to go wrong before they are at screaming pitch with one another and the children. I asked them to describe to me what might happen on a typical 'bad' morning and to describe their *feelings* as that morning went on...

They described how, one night recently, they had gone to bed and forgotten to set the alarm clock. As daylight flooded the bedroom and they woke up nearly an hour late ("What total *idiots* we are") they hurtled out of bed. Rhiannon was already screaming at Laura and Christopher to get up *quickly* ("Why can't they hurry just *once*?"). With no time to shower or choose clean clothes, David threw on yesterday's things ("I look a *wreck*. I'm *never* going to get promoted"). He could hear Rhiannon still shouting at the children to eat up breakfast and get into the car (he says he felt, "I should earn more so she doesn't have to work". She says she felt, "This is *all* my fault. My kids will *hate* me"). As they herded their now upset and anxious kids, plus their unwashed sports kits, into the car ("We are *awful parents*") they both said they had felt defeated ("The day is *ruined*").

Ring any bells? Do you feel tense and anxious just *reading* it? But was there any alternative, given that the alarm wasn't set and they were all going to be late? I pointed out to them that at various stages of that one hour in the morning their self-mottos had been something along the lines of *'We are idiotic, badly dressed, unwashed, unloving parents'* and they instantly agreed! I asked them if feeling this awful actually helped the situation. They both said, "No! It just made everything even worse!" Both of them had gone on to have a bad day at work too.

So I asked them if they felt 'bullied' by the huge pressures they were under to bring up their small children and earn enough money to pay off a substantial mortgage. They were agreed on their answer, "We do. But we also know it was our choice to have the children and buy a bigger house." Over our session I asked them to take on board the fact that even though it was their choice, we could all see that it was very hard work and they were entitled to feel upset and angry that this was such a difficult task. But having accepted that, they now needed to summon up some positive energy to decide what it was they actually *wanted* to happen. They were agreed on this too! They both said, "We want our kids to grow up feeling we love them and enjoy them!" So I asked them one more question, "Do you think that changing how you felt about what happened and changing your self-mottos would have made any difference?" And while we're on the subject, could it even make a difference to the way *you* feel about these parents?

I asked them to imagine that they had still forgotten to set the alarm. As daylight flooded the bedroom they still woke up late but this time they congratulated themselves on getting a decent night's sleep for once (*"Wow! Neither of the kids woke us up in the night! We slept really well"*). Still late but feeling pleased about the night's uninterrupted sleep, they ask Laura and Christopher to get up quickly (*"What stars you were sleeping through the night!"*). Still too late to shower, they still have to throw on yesterday's clothes (*"Life's too short to worry about one day without a shower! It's more important to give the kids a good breakfast"*). And finally, still late, they all jump into the car (*"With any luck we'll only be a bit late! How clever are we?"*) The unwashed sports kit is still thrown into the boot (*"We'll be really organised and wash that lot tonight"*)!

Sounds too good to be true? But what a huge difference it made! Note that their self-mottos were, at various points, *"We are rested parents with great kids who sleep through the night"* plus *"We care more about the really important things in life"* and *"Despite everything we're still only a little bit late!"* and even, *"We're really clever!"* And the difference won't have just changed the way they felt about themselves – how did *you* feel reading it? Admit it! You were at least a *bit* impressed and certainly less stressed on their behalf! And most important of all, what they had originally wanted – to let Laura and Christopher feel wanted and loved despite the pressures of a tight schedule – was *exactly* what they achieved!

It's fairly easy to accept that the way we feel about ourselves affects how we personally behave. What's harder to accept – but is equally true – is that *others are also reacting to the way we silently feel about ourselves because how we feel about ourselves affects the way that they react to us!*

And how does this link to your child getting bullied?

Over the years I've been lucky enough to discuss this idea about self-motto with hundreds and hundreds of children and those that say they are being bullied have one big thing in common. *They do not feel good about themselves* (they have a negative self-motto which means they have low self-esteem).

Immediately I can hear you say that your child is much loved and that you are at pains to let them know this. *And* you constantly reassure them about their undoubted strengths. I have no doubt whatsoever that this is absolutely true. Unfortunately this is not the only reassurance that children need. They have a self-motto based on their own feelings of self-worth and this will only *partly* be determined by what you feel about them. Their self-esteem will *also* be based on their teacher's view of them, the views of other kids in their class and the views of everyone else they meet in the course of a day.

So you can see that telling them how much you love them and how wonderful they are at drawing / sums / writing stories / swimming will only have a positive affect on some of their self-esteem. What they also need to build on is genuine high self-esteem about their relationships with a variety of other people.

Since you are going to help them with this, we'll set off with you doing the exercise first...

Exercise 1:

First I want you to imagine this... You too woke late, but still found time to get on the scales (you're on a diet but somehow you've *gained* three pounds). The trousers you wanted to wear are in the wash and the tracksuit bottoms you're left with will make you look *hideous*. You too have forgotten to wash the kids' gym kit and you suspect that their teacher notices these things and will now disapprove of you... Worst of all, you have a meeting with this teacher to discuss your child's (you suspect poor) progress this morning!

I want you to write down how you feel about yourself (your negative self-motto!) as you enter the classroom. To make this exercise work at its best, imagine yourself at your *very worst*! Really go to town on this and let your imagination run riot!

I feel…

Bearing in mind that this negative self-motto will affect how you actually look, tell me about your body language (things like your facial expression and how likely you are to make eye contact with people). What about your hands – are they clenched, or are you wringing them? What about your shoulders – are they all hunched up? And how do you behave – do you stride up to see the teacher or do you hang back hoping he/she won't notice you?

My facial expression?

My body language?

How am I likely to behave?

Now tell me how your body language, based on your silent, negative self-motto, will affect *how the teacher is likely to react to you.*

He/she will probably...

Last of all, how does his/her reaction to you now make you feel – better about yourself or worse about yourself?

Whether you went in with all guns blazing (I feel... "It's none of your damn business how I look *or* whether the gym kit is washed!") or feeling grim (I am... "Fat, badly dressed and disorganised!"), how you *felt* about yourself (your self-motto) would have shown in your face and your body language. If you felt angry, this would have been pretty obvious – you were probably frowning with your jaw pushed forward. You might have stared aggressively, with your shoulders up and your hands clenched. You might have looked quite scary! But if the situation just made you feel miserable, your head would have been down, with little or no eye contact. Your shoulders might have been hunched and your hands tucked into your pockets. Admit it, you would have looked a pushover, wouldn't you?

We're not talking right or wrong here, we're just recognising that either way the teacher would have subconsciously noticed your body language and reacted accordingly. That's because this is what brains are actually programmed to do – be subconsciously alert to any possible threat. If the teacher notes that you are angry, he/she may well react aggressively or they may run away to the staff room! Equally, if he/she notes that you think you're of little worth, the possibility is that they will simply accept that and either pity you or ignore you. And how will any of those reactions make you feel? *Even worse about yourself!*

Try this again and watch how you change the outcome!

Exercise 2:

We always need to go through Strategies 1 and 2 first!

- *Bullying?* – Well, *do* you feel a bit bullied by this situation / teacher? Recognising that you probably do means that you can now accept it and move straight on to dealing with it in a positive way!
- *Stop&Think!* What do you actually want to happen at this meeting? Do you want to score points over this teacher so that they now feel inferior to you? Or do you just want to have a good meeting so that you and the teacher can help your child to achieve their full potential?
- *Self-motto* We've seen what a negative one can do! Let's try again and change the outcome...

You still woke late and got on the scales ("Hooray! Despite that huge blowout last night, I only gained three pounds – and most of that will be water-retention!") The trousers you wanted to wear are in the wash ("If I team the tracksuit bottoms that are left with a baggy T-shirt and trainers, at least it'll look as if I find time to jog before school"). Still no time to wash the kids' gym kit ("Who really has time to notice these things?"). And still you have a meeting with the teacher this morning to discuss your child's progress ("My kids do their best most of the time. It's probably fine")...

Well, aren't you the star! Based on this, I want you to write down how you NOW feel about yourself (your positive self-motto) as you re-enter the classroom (the clues are in the text!).

I now feel...

Bearing in mind that this new, positive self-motto will affect how you actually look, tell me about your facial expressions (are you smiling and making eye contact?). What about your body language (are your shoulders back and your hands relaxed?). What about the way you behave? Do you now go forward positively and expect a fair summing up of your child's progress?

My facial expression now?

My body language now?

How do I now behave?

Tell me how *your* body language, based on your positive, silent self-motto, will affect how the teacher is now likely to react to you...

He/she will probably...

Last of all, *how does this new reaction, based on your new, positive self-motto, make you feel about yourself?* Better or worse?

Brilliant! I bet you felt so much more powerful and energetic about the whole thing. If you too are someone who finds it difficult to feel good about themselves when the chips are down, start writing a list of all the things that you *like* about yourself and even all the things you would like to be. So whenever you feel anxious about one of life's events (meeting new people, public speaking) bring out one of your "I am intelligent, friendly, nice to hamsters" kind of self-mottos – and repeat it silently in your head for as long as it takes for your nerves to subside! It won't just make *you* feel better, it'll make other people respond to you better too! And more importantly, if what you originally wanted was a positive meeting in which you and your child's teacher were able to discuss the best ways to help your child... you will have succeeded!

In your child's chapter on this, there are two exercises for you to practise with them. The first one is not personal so that neither of you will find it threatening. The second one is an experiment that cuts to the chase and helps your child to examine their own self-motto.

So now you have THREE positive anti-bullying strategies to help your child stop the bullying that's happening to them!

1. BULLYING? Is it *only teasing* or is it actual bullying? It doesn't matter *what* you call it – it still makes you feel wretched and it still needs sorting out.

2. STOP&THINK! What do you want to be the *outcome* of this sorting out? Do you want to score points? Or do you want to achieve something positive for your child?

3. SELF-MOTTO Changing a negative self-motto to a positive one raises self-esteem. It not only changes the way you feel about yourself – it changes the way other people see you too!

What's in it for you?

Now you know how to do it, you can teach your child this vital, energising life skill. They will then be able to see that there is a rock solid connection between the way they feel about themselves and the way others react to them...

- *Negative self-mottos can be spotted in negative body language and behaviour – and attract negative responses (bullying).*

- *Positive self-mottos can be spotted in positive body language and behaviour – and attract positive responses (respect).*

Kids – Chapter 2

Can you stop thinking? Absolutely not think about *anything*? Test yourself – get a watch with a second hand and for ONE minute – STOP THINKING!

What happened? Did you do it? Or did you start thinking about how long you had to go, or if you had to hold your breath, or stop your eyelids blinking? What about sounds you heard like somebody's annoying music, or the cat fussing about how long it was since breakfast? Did you wish you'd put on a sweatshirt first because you could feel a breeze?

Unless you're dead (don't go there!) it's *impossible* not to think. It's as if there is a part of you inside your brain that is talking away and never shuts up! Incidentally, this voice inside your brain, that only you can hear, is where you think secret thoughts about yourself. And the actual words you use to describe yourself I'm going to call your SELF-MOTTO. Your self-motto (the way you think about yourself) changes throughout the day as you do different things or you're with different people.

For instance, you *might* secretly think you are the best person in your class at spelling (Self-motto = 'I am a great speller'). Would it be a good idea to stand up in class and tell everybody you think this? Probably NOT! After all, what if you were wrong and everyone laughed at you? Or if everyone thought you were a total show-off? So even if you thought you were the best you would probably decide not to tell everyone and to keep this self-motto secret.

But the big question is, *are* your secret feelings about yourself (your self-motto) *actually* secret? Actually, no! Why? Because *how we feel about ourselves shows up in the way we look and how we behave*. So if your self-motto is 'I am brilliant at spelling' and the teacher asks you to spell something, because you feel very confident at getting it right this will show in the way you look and act. You'll probably be smiling and look confidently at the teacher as you answer.

What's more, because you secretly feel confident, the teacher will be expecting a good answer and will probably be smiling back at you. I wonder if the teacher's self-motto is 'You are good because I am such a brilliant teacher.' Also, based on your confident look, the rest of the class will be expecting you to do well and they should be looking confident too (*their* self-motto might be = 'we are a great class because one of us can spell this word!').

But what if you secretly think you can't spell (self-motto = 'I'm rubbish at spelling')? How do you think you will answer now? Will you look really worried, stare at the floor and say the answer quietly in case you're wrong? How might the teacher look now? Worried as well? (Teacher's self-motto = 'Oh no! What if they all do badly in SATs?') And what about the rest of the class? Might they be sniggering because you look like you can't do it (*their* self-motto = 'I hope the teacher doesn't ask me! I'm rubbish at spelling too!').

And if you can understand why this whole thing is important, this is excellent thinking on your part and worth *at least* TWENTY gold stars. Because you now understand that:

- *The way you secretly think about yourself* (your self-motto) *makes a difference to how you look and behave.*
- *Your personal self-motto ALSO affects how other people think about you!*

GOOD! Now that's sorted, I'd be really interested to see what you think this boy called Max might be saying about himself (his self-motto) and how this might affect how Max behaves – and how he gets treated.

Exercise 1

Max thinks he is rubbish at gym classes. Every time he has to climb wall bars, or ropes, he gets worried and tense. Because his body is so tense he often falls over / off! This makes him feel *even* worse about climbing. His friends used to say, "Bad luck, Max" but then he felt embarrassed and looked the other way. So they started to ignore him if he fell. Now he feels *worse still* because he's pretty sure that not only does he look stupid, but also that nobody even cares that he has hurt himself. So instead of being part of his old group of mates, Max stands by himself in the gym these days. Based on what you've just read about him, what do you think Max's *miserable* self-motto probably is?

I am...

What clues do you think he would have given away in his facial expressions about his self-motto? Do you think he might have been frowning, or looking as if he was about to cry? Anything else?

-
-
-

What about the way his body looks (his body language) and the way he behaves? (Things like looking his friends in the eye or facing away from them) Can you think of anything else?

-
-
-

Now write out how you think the way Max behaves (because of his self-motto) might change the way that his friends treat him...

They might...

Last of all, I want you to write in if Max's self-motto (and the effect it has on his friends) makes him feel *better* about himself or even *worse* about himself?

He feels ＿＿＿＿＿＿＿ about himself!

Another TEN gold stars if you put in that his self-motto made him look as if he didn't want his friends. And that once they started leaving him alone he felt *even worse* about himself.

I want to ask you a question: How easy do you think it is for Max to just change his self-motto? Please try the next exercise before you decide!

Exercise 2
This is ferociously difficult, so take a deep breath and concentrate HARD!

I want you NOT to imagine a huge pink elephant coming through your kitchen door riding a wobbly blue bicycle!

Remember! *This is very important!*

PLEASE DO **NOT** IMAGINE A **HUGE** PINK ELEPHANT COMING THROUGH YOUR KITCHEN DOOR RIDING A **WOBBLY** BLUE BICYCLE! DO NOT EVEN *THINK* ABOUT HIS FLOPPY PINK **EARS**, HIS **CUTE** LITTLE PINK TRUNK, OR HIS **TINY** BLACK EYES...

Did you do it? NOT think of a huge pink elephant riding through your kitchen door on a wobbly blue bicycle? Did you shut out all thoughts of floppy pink ears, cute pink trunk and tiny black eyes?

NO, YOU DID NOT! Because as soon as you *think* a thing *it's there in your head!* And EXACTLY the same thing happens if we decide to change our self-motto. Once we have thought we are OK, we suddenly feel a whole lot better about ourselves!

Let's quickly prove it by looking at Max again...

Max knows he isn't as good as his mates at gym classes. But every time he has to climb ropes / wall bars at least he has a positive self-motto. Something like "This time I'll try really hard – and if I fall it's no big deal." He tries... and he falls! But his self-motto reminds him this is not the end of the world. When his friends shout over, "Bad luck, Max!" he laughs with them and says, "Thanks!" They are impressed that he keeps trying!

Now Max feels so much more cheerful, what is his positive (but still secret) self-motto?

I am...

And how does this self-motto show in his face and his behaviour?

-
-

How does Max's self-motto and behaviour change the way that his friends treat him?

-

Last of all, I want you to write in if the way Max's friends now treat him made him feel *better* about himself or *worse* about himself?

He feels _____ about himself!

IMPORTANT...

You're reading this book because YOU want the bullying to stop happening to YOU.

You need to have a look at what YOU might be secretly saying about *yourself* and how this will affect how YOU look and behave!

And then what effect you think your self-motto has on other people!

Sound complicated?

NO! Let's just get on with it and make it really easy...

How do you find out what your self-motto is and how it affects the way other people treat you?

Easy! We'll just do another quick scientific experiment so that you can understand what it is about YOU that bullies enjoy getting a rise out of...

What exactly is a scientific experiment?

Well, this kind comes in four simple parts:

- First, you describe the problem (your *Introduction*).

56

- Second, you decide what *you* might do to solve it (your *Method*).
- Third, you look at what happened when you carried out the solving part (this part is called your *Results*).
- Lastly, you decide what you think the results actually mean (and this is called your *Conclusions*).

Experiment 1
Introduction:

You have been told that you can do your favourite thing this Saturday. You choose a day at a theme park (Alton Towers perhaps?) and you are getting all ready and excited when your parents suddenly turn round and say, "We've decided that we won't let you do that after all. Because you are so far behind in class, you're going to do extra schoolwork instead! Get out your school books."

Method:

1. Decide what your silent self-motto is likely to be! Something like, 'I am angry and upset and stupid' (this is called a *negative* self-motto).
2. Spend some time thinking how angry, upset and stupid you are (maybe ten minutes). Stomp around a bit and let people know how you feel!
3. After the ten minutes are up, make a note of how other people treated you whilst you were doing your stomping!

Results:

Even though you didn't say what you were feeling, did other people seem irritable with you? Did you get the feeling they were not on your side? And did that make you feel even *more* cross, or *worse* about yourself?

Conclusions:

If you felt *worse*, you were the *same* as all the other people who have done this experiment because they too said that they felt a lot worse about themselves after they did it! This means that:

If we secretly feel bad about ourselves (we have a negative self-motto) those secret feelings will show in the way we look and behave.

The negative way we look and behave (based on our secret, negative self-motto) will affect the way that other people treat us!

WELL DONE! Now on to Experiment 2
Introduction:

Your parents have just told you that because you've done brilliantly at school this week you can go out wherever you choose and celebrate! What will it be for you? Hang out with friends? Football match? Nude rock climbing? How are you secretly feeling about yourself now? Is your self-motto something like 'I am pleased, happy and extremely clever' by any chance? I'm not surprised!

Method:

Again, without telling anybody what your secret feelings are about this, I want you to spend another ten minutes thinking about just how pleased, happy and extremely clever you are (this is called a *positive* self-motto)! And as you hang around people, I want you to notice how they treat you... and whether you being cheerful makes a difference to this...

Results:

Even though you didn't let on what your self-motto is ('I am pleased, happy and extremely clever!'), did you think they were nicer to you than last time (when you secretly felt angry, disappointed and stupid)? And based on the way they treated you this time, did you now feel even *better* about yourself?

Conclusions:

If you felt better about yourself, you were like all the other people who have done this experiment. When they had a positive self-motto (felt really good about themselves), they also felt they were treated better and this made them feel even happier about themselves. Finding this out makes us see that *if we have a strong, positive self-motto it will show in the way we look and behave. And this will affect the way that other people treat us!*

Of course, on a deeper level what it means is that people treat us the way we look as if we *expect* to be treated. Which is a scary thought if you had been thinking that either:

- no one knew how you felt about yourself
- People could see you looked fed-up so would be nicer to you

Here are the rules for if you are about to get bullied:
1. Think about what your self-motto is at this exact moment...
2. Remember pink elephants (to remind you that you can change the way you think).
3. Quickly give yourself a strong, positive self-motto that helps you to feel good about yourself – *and keep thinking it!*

Keep doing this to remind yourself how a positive self-motto will actually give out clues to other people to help them be nice to you! By the way, sometimes we find it hard to think of anything good about ourselves when we're being picked on, so here is a list of strong, positive words that you might like to choose from if you're a bit stuck! You can choose any that you think you *are* or any that you would *like* to be – have fun!

A – ambitious, amazing, adventurous

B – *bold, brave, bouncy, brilliant, beautiful, balanced*

C – creative, calm, confident, clever, considerate, caring

D – deserving, discovering, dreamy, delightful, determined

E – energetic, exciting, enthusiastic, extraordinary, excited

F – fun, friendly, funny, fantastic, fascinating, fortunate, forgiving

G – growing, giving, good, glad, grateful, generous, gentle, giggly

H – happy, healthy, helpful, high-spirited

I – intelligent, imaginative, investigating

JK – jolly, knowledgeable, kind, keen

L – laughing, loving, learning, leader, lively, lucky, loveable

MN – motivated, marvellous, modest, mysterious, natural, nice

O – optimistic, observant, organised

P – positive, peaceful, precious, playful, persuasive, polite, praising, proud, private

Q R – quick, quiet, relaxed, responsible, reasonable, restful

S – singing, smiling, strong, safe, secure, sensible, sunny, successful, sociable, sympathetic, surprising

T – talented, terrific, trusting, thinking, trustworthy

UV – unique, useful, unpredictable, valuable

W, X, Y, Z – wonderful, warm, wild, wise, winning, worthwhile, Xtra-special, young, zippy

So you now have THREE brilliant strategies ready to help you cope with bullies!

1. BULLYING?
    Is it bullying or is it just teasing? YOU know that if you feel bullied you have been – even if the person didn't mean to upset you. And you now know you have to do something positive about yourself fast to make yourself feel better!

2. STOP&THINK!
    You also know that you have to be sure what you want to happen in the end. If you want other kids / teachers / parents to like you, you need to be extra careful about what you do to sort stuff out.

3. SELF-MOTTO

Remember! *Most kids bully because they have found that each time they put someone else down, they feel a bit better about themselves.* When they feel low, they start looking for that person who looks easy to put down. Now you know that if you *feel* sad and frightened, you probably *look* sad and frightened. So you will quickly realise that the bully will see you as one of those easy targets! They put you down... and feel better. And you feel even worse. So get a store of strong, positive self-mottos ready, fast! Use them and enjoy them!

IMPORTANT...

Nobody but YOU can make you really confident about yourself or give you high self-esteem.

You have to do it for yourself.

And now you know how!

ADULTS – CHAPTER 3

OTHER-MOTTO

Technical bit:

You've probably heard of 'self-fulfilling prophecies'. Or the phrase, 'Give a dog a bad name and...' What both these statements are saying is, 'If you expect a certain behaviour you will probably find it'. This explains why teachers who say to their students, "You are the worst class I teach all week!" will find them as disruptive and difficult to control as they had feared. And equally, why teachers who say, "I've been looking forward to seeing you lot all day because you're such a great class!" will find a far more willing group! If you and your child view the bully as 'the-thug-from-hell' this will have implications for what happens...

Example:

Personally, I used to think I had the mother-in-law from hell! She didn't seem to think I was anything like good enough for her son, and she also seemed at pains to let me know this! I adopted a somewhat aggressive self-motto (something along the lines of "I'm younger, *far* nicer and it's me he wants to be with", since you ask). So why did my teeth grind horribly together each time she said something like "The pudding was OK, but one day you must let me show you how to make *nice* custard". (Please tell me your teeth are clenched at that too and it's not just me!) I was furious. I lay in bed plotting how to come up with the perfect put-down ("Oh, I *can* make good custard. I just never get time for that with your son always wanting my attention..." etc. etc.)

I made my husband's life miserable too ("Why do you *never* support me?", "I'm beginning to wonder who you love most!"). Yes, I *know* that's below the belt and pathetic and divided his loyalties. But that's the trouble when we feel bullied. If we feel humiliated and we can't deal with it, we start to feel isolated. And once that happens we do one or both of two things:

- We change our self-motto ("I'm not as great as I thought and he doesn't want to be with me enough to defend me")
- We enlist help by telling all our friends ("You will never *guess* what my mother-in-law has said now..." etc.)

OK, so I dragged a new self-motto out of myself despite the odds ("I am loved and loving"). But did it stop my teeth grinding each time a *new* 'insult' came my way? NO IT DID NOT! Despite my new, strong self-motto, on occasion my mother-in-law and I were still heading for all-out warfare!

Eventually I realised that my real problem was in the way I thought about her. I attributed to her a power she didn't actually have – or probably, in all honesty, actually want. And worse still, by thinking of her as "possessive, powerful and determined to keep her son away from me", I felt unable to cope. If the truth were known, I'm pretty sure I looked and behaved like a sulky teenager! No wonder she continued to put me down – I made such a wonderful, responsive target.

I tried another tack. I *finally* realised that in order to deal with her I needed to *change the way I thought about her*. Because the way I thought about her affected the way I behaved almost as much as my self-motto did. I realised that I needed some sort of motto for the way I thought about her too. An 'other-motto' perhaps?

Interestingly, once I thought of her in terms of attributes that I admire ("she's loving, protective and a good cook") I *instantly* had far fewer problems. For a start, once I realised we had things I value in common I stopped sulking around her! I asked her about her cooking skills, and I *even* acknowledged that she loved her son and wanted the best for him! She began to talk to me as if we were allies. I began to like her. She, I like to think, began to like me. We *never* agreed on everything! But we did, finally, respect one another and, eventually, come to love one another. She died many years ago but I still think of her with great fondness and respect.

When the teenagers I worked with heard about this, they too tried it out. And they too found it was successful! We added it to the list of useful strategies and when I taught it to other children *they* liked it too! They said it helped because when they can only hate bullies they can't sort things out! And they're absolutely right. If we only think in black and white terms, we can only come up with black and white solutions. Which is a bit limited, isn't it?

A lovely mum I was once asked to help, called Sonia, has a daughter, Maisie. Maisie attends the local primary school. A bright six-year-old, Maisie started her school life already able to read and write. Sonia assumed that this would impress Maisie's new teacher and was surprised when her daughter came out of school saying that her teacher was often cross with her for being stupid. Sonia felt, quite rightly, that she should investigate. She made an appointment to see this teacher. And then, just as she was walking through the playground to that appointment, she heard Maisie's teacher's voice through an open window. "Maisie! What *are* you doing now? You're supposed to be such a clever girl and yet here is everyone ready for break-time except you! Stop messing about this instant and get ready like everyone else, you stupid girl!" Sonia's back was understandably up! How *dare* the teacher refer to her daughter as stupid? Obviously this teacher was unfair, unkind and unpleasant – and I suspect most of us can sympathise over what happened next...

Sonia felt no difficulty in going in to class and telling the teacher *exactly* how she felt about her! Instead of backing down, the teacher was now outraged too! She pressed the 'panic' button under her desk and, when other teachers came racing into the classroom, demanded that they escort this aggressive and unreasonable parent from her classroom! The head teacher, on hearing Sonia's fury at Maisie's teacher, suggested that unless she could be reasonable about this, she, Sonia, may well be banned from coming into school again! Sonia left the school in a total rage, determined to get the school governors on her side. She made another appointment!

What we are all hoping here (since we know Sonia's side of this story) is that the school governors asked Maisie's teacher to give a full apology for her derogatory remarks to one of her charges. But you know, and I know, that people who are backed into a corner rarely give us what we really want. However in the wrong she had been, Maisie's teacher now also felt she had been threatened. Not only that, she had been threatened publicly, in front of her own class! The other teachers in the school (who were told that the comments to Maisie had been said in a light, jokey voice and that Maisie had been smiling back happily) also now felt threatened by Sonia. The school governors, therefore, backed up the head teacher. Sonia eventually came to me with Maisie because even though Sonia was sure she was in the right she still couldn't sort it out.

Bullying? First we looked at whether we thought the teacher was bullying Maisie. We decided that however the teacher felt, Maisie was upset and certainly *felt* bullied. So Sonia and Maisie both needed to summon up lots of positive energy to help sort things out.

Stop&Think! Next we talked about what outcome Maisie (and Sonia) wanted. Maisie wanted the teacher not to call her stupid and Sonia wanted that *and* an apology.

Self-Motto We needed to do some work on changing Maisie's self-motto which turned out to be "My teacher doesn't like me. I probably am stupid." She chose to change it to "I'm good at reading and I like seeing all my friends at school." Sonia's had been "I care intensely about my daughter's happiness" and she wanted to stick with this.

Other-Motto Last of all we looked at both their other-mottos for Maisie's teacher (both now veered towards "unfair, unkind and unpleasant!"). We examined what effect this had had on their interaction with her. Even though it had a degree of accuracy (the teacher had, at the very least, behaved insensitively) I again asked Sonia what she had really wanted from this meeting. She replied that she had wanted the teacher to understand that her daughter found her, the teacher, a bit scary and could she be a bit gentler in her remarks to her? Which is a perfectly reasonable request. And it is entirely possible that had Sonia not heard the teacher shouting, she may have achieved this aim.

The secondary problem was that Sonia now had negative other-mottos for everyone involved in banning her from the school too! What Sonia and I now had to work through was what Sonia now wanted from *this* situation. She thought about it for some while and replied that she still wanted an apology from the class teacher. However, like her daughter, Sonia is clever. She did recognise that she'd gone about it the wrong way. So I asked her to simply re-phrase the other-mottos she had about the school governors, the head teacher and the class teacher! We agreed that the values she assigned to them had to be ones that she personally found attractive.

We started with the governors and the head teacher, as they were easier. Instead of feeling they hadn't listened to her and didn't care about her child, she came up with "They are loyal to their colleague", and "They are protective of all the children if they think they might be threatened by any parent". These statements made a profound difference to the letter she then wrote to them asking if she could 'start again' and talk to somebody about what she thought was a problem affecting her little girl. She got her appointment.

Sonia and I then quickly did some more work on her other-motto for the teacher before her meeting. I asked Sonia to find out from Maisie all the things Maisie *did* like about her class. Maisie was happy to say that in her class they did fantastic nature studies with this same teacher who brought in all sorts of things she had found to excite their interest. She also liked listening to the stories that her teacher told at the end of the day because they were really exciting. Sonia was now gaining a more rounded picture of this teacher. Did it mean she probably hadn't been bullying after all towards Maisie? No! It did not! But it meant there were also some very positive points to work with.

Sonia went to her meeting. The chair of the board of governors, the head teacher and the class teacher were all there. It could have felt quite intimidating! Sonia started off her remarks just as we'd agreed. She apologised for her outburst in front of the whole class and explained what she thought she'd heard from the playground. She said that Maisie had told her about the wonderful nature studies this teacher did, and how she read fantastic stories at the end of the school day. But Maisie also was a little afraid of the teacher because the teacher sometimes called her stupid and Maisie didn't understand why. This combination of positive remarks as well as stating the case meant that everyone understood the problem *and* felt less threatened. The teacher was surprisingly quick to apologise and admit that she *did* expect more from Maisie than from the other children just because she was so bright.

Essentially the problem was sorted. Sonia had stuck to her guns about the teacher's behaviour being bullying rather than 'just a little teasing' and she had used the STOP&THINK! strategy to decide what outcome she eventually wanted (for Maisie to be happier at school). Her self-motto had remained steady – that she cared intensely about her daughter's happiness. The only things that she had really had to change were her other-mottos. Not easy! But she was so glad that she'd made the effort because eventually she did get what she'd wanted – the teacher was more careful in her remarks and Maisie settled into school easily.

What about *your* 'other-mottos'? How do *you* feel, for instance, about the child who is bullying yours? Something along the lines of, "Vicious, unpleasant and foul-mouthed"? I see you're not one to beat about the bush! But tell me, whilst you think these things, how does this other-motto affect the way *you* behave? Do you, even whilst thinking it, feel that you are frowning, your jaw is pushed forward and your mouth is clamped firmly shut? Well you're frightening me at any rate! And will this small thug now back down and admit that they may have behaved badly? You're absolutely right, no they will not! They will now, in point of fact, only feel bullied themselves (by you!) and feel the need to get *more* people on their side to dislike your child as well... And will that make *you* feel better? Unless you are one of those people who enjoy a flat-out war, I rather suspect not! And certainly not when you fear for the safety and happiness of your child.

I need you to do a really difficult exercise. Indeed, it is probably the hardest one in this entire book. I need you to think of *three* things about this child who bullies yours that you could admire if only they were *not* bullying your child. A *positive* 'other-motto'. Just in case this is really horribly difficult, I'm throwing in a few useful examples of positive words. But only use them if they are qualities you personally admire or it won't make a real difference to the outcome!

A – ambitious, amazing, adventurous, achieving, alert, amusing, attractive, able, absorbing, awesome, accomplished

B – bold, brave, blissful, bouncy, brilliant, beautiful, balanced, broadminded, bright

C – centred, creative, committed, calm, confident, constructive, clever, captivating, considerate, communicative, compassionate, courageous, cherished, charismatic, caring

D – deserving, dynamic, direct, discovering, dreamy, delightful, dedicated, devoted, determined

E – energetic, exciting, enthusiastic, extraordinary, effective, excited, extraverted, easy-going, enterprising, educated, experienced, empowered, empowering,

F – friendly, funny, fabulous, faithful, fantastic, fascinating, fashionable, focused, fortunate, forgiving, forthright

G – growing, glowing, glittering, giving, good, great, golden, genuine, giggly, glamorous, glad, grateful, generous, gentle

H – happy, healthy, headstrong, healing, helpful, humble, honourable, high-spirited, high-flying, humorous

I – inspiring, inquisitive, intelligent, impulsive, imaginative, impressive, independent, intriguing, investigating, inspirational

JK – jolly, joyful, just, knowledgeable, kind, keen

L – laughing, loving, learning, leading, lively, lovely, lucky, loveable, logical

M – motivated, marvellous, miraculous, modest, mysterious, magnetic, meticulous, magnificent, merciful, merry, meek, mature, methodical

N – natural, noble, nice, nourishing, nimble

O – original, optimistic, open-minded, obliging, observant, organised

P – positive, passionate, powerful, peaceful, precious, playful, phenomenal, perceptive, persuasive, pioneering, plucky, polite, praising, privileged, proud, private, promising

QR – quick, quiet, quirky, radiant, relaxed, resourceful, responsible, rational, recovering, reasonable, reassuring, restful

S – singing, smiling, sparkling, supportive, stylish, splendid, searching, sincere, strong, secure, sensible, sunny, serene, successful, sociable, spontaneous, stimulating, subtle, sympathetic, surprising

T – *talented, terrific, trusting, thinking, tolerant, thankful, thrilling, trustworthy*

UV – unique, useful, unpretentious, unpredictable, vivacious, victorious, vibrant, vital, valuable, virtuous

WXYZ – wonderful, warm, wild, wise, winning, wholesome, worthwhile, wacky, winning, witty, Xtra-special, young, zippy

Now write in three of those positive words *with values that you personally find valuable*, below!

I may find it hard to admit, but this bully is also…

Feel the words you have just written. How do they affect the way you hold yourself when you think of the bully? How do they affect your facial expression and body language? Or how you feel you might now behave when you see them again?

- My face / body language now...

- My behaviour now...

How is the bully likely to respond to you, with your new, positive *other*-motto affecting how you are now looking and behaving?

- They are likely to...

And how does their new reaction to you make you feel about yourself? More, or less, in control? Better or worse about yourself?

- I now feel...

Please tell me you felt better about yourself! The thing is, we are *far* more likely to sort out problems with people we have something (*anything!*) in common with. This is why it was important that you wrote down positive things that you personally admire rather than just any old positive words. It takes real courage to go forward in this way rather than descend to their level.

And now you have FOUR positive anti-bullying strategies to help your child stop the bullying that's happening to them!

1. BULLYING? Is it *teasing* or bullying? It doesn't matter which you call it – if it makes us feel wretched, it needs sorting out.

2. STOP&THINK! What do you want to be the *outcome* of this sorting out? Do you want to score points? Or do you want to achieve something positive for your child?

3. SELF-MOTTO Changing a negative self-motto to a positive one raises self-esteem. It not only changes the way you *feel* about yourself – it changes the way other people treat you too.

4. OTHER-MOTTO Changing the way you feel about others to include positive things *also* raises your self-esteem. It reminds you that you have the power to change how you feel about any person or situation. And that feeling more positive about others makes it easier to sort out the bullying – which is what you wanted all along.

What's in it for you?
Who, or what, else do you sometimes feel bullied by? How will you use what you now know to sort that out successfully too? What effect will you doing that have on your child? Good, isn't it?

Kids - Chapter 3

How do you actually *feel* about the bully?

Is the person who is bullying you someone you hardly ever speak to?

Or did they use to be your friend?

Are you scared of them?

Or just really angry with them?

Do you think that how you feel about them makes any difference to what's happening?

Well, most of what we know about how people behave comes from scientists doing experiments on how people behave and then letting the rest of us know what they found. So! Back into your white coat, sunshine! Before I can give you the next really useful strategy you need to be the scientist again first and discover exactly how YOU feel about this one.

First a warm-up experiment to give you some practise...

Experiment number 1

Introduction:

Sam used to be best friends with you.
You used to hang out together all the
time because you liked doing the same
things. But at the start of term Jamie
starts in your class and the teacher gets your friend
Sam to look after Jamie. Pretty soon you find that Sam
and Jamie are now best friends and you are being left
out all the time. You try being friendly but they go off
together and don't invite you to anything. You try
asking Sam what's the matter, but Sam says, "Nothing!
Don't fuss!" You feel really upset. And you feel lonely
too. Worse still, Sam and Jamie now start laughing as
they walk past you. You're pretty sure that they are
laughing AT you. You begin to really HATE Jamie for
taking Sam away from you.

If the way you feel about yourself is called a *self-
motto*, the way you feel about someone else is called an
OTHER-MOTTO. We now know (from the
experiments you did earlier) that your self-motto
(your *secret* feelings about yourself) can actually affect
what then happens to you. This is because your
private feelings affect the way you look. And the way
you look affects how other people see you and decide
to treat you.

What we now need to see is:

Does the secret way you feel about *someone else* also
affect what happens?

Method:

Decide on how you would feel about Jamie as if this was happening to you. Write down your secret feelings about Jamie (your *other-motto*). You are allowed to be really horrible here and say something like, "Jamie is mean and selfish and I hate Jamie!"

• Jamie is...

Now decide how this other-motto affects how you *look* and how you *behave*. (This might be something like, "I look really fierce and I give Sam and Jamie angry looks". And, "I sit far away from Sam and Jamie at lunch-time now and sometimes I start laughing at *Jamie* as Sam and Jamie walk past *me!*")

• How I look (clues above!)...

• How I behave (even more clues above!)...

Results:

What do YOU expect happened when Sam and Jamie saw you giving them bad looks? How do you think they felt about you when you laughed at them (or perhaps you ran away to the teacher, crying)? Even though you didn't actually *say* what your other-motto was, do you think that Sam and Jamie probably thought you didn't like them now? Might this have made them think perhaps it was OK now to leave you out of things? And say that because you laughed at them, now they could tell everyone how mean and nasty YOU are? Write in how they might NOW treat you.

- They now...

Would the way they now treat you make you feel *better* about yourself, or *worse* about yourself?

- I would feel... _____ about myself!

Conclusions:

The way we secretly feel about other people (our other-motto) *does* seem to affect what happens to us. Other people pick up clues from the way that we look (and this includes our body language). They then treat us well, or badly, based on those clues. We don't need to *say* anything! Feeling bad about someone else can make that person even meaner to us. This then makes us feel even worse about ourselves and about them. *Worst of all, this makes us MUCH less able to sort out the problem.*

Experiment number 2

Time for the real thing... After all, YOU might need to sort out the odd bullying problem of your own! I want you to do the same experiment but this time I want you to write in *what's happened to you* and how you feel about the person who has bullied you. Remember you can say how you *really* feel here. You can be as nasty as you like – in fact it helps the experiment if you do! Of course you can always leave out the name of the bully in case you become friends again and they find this book on your shelves!

Introduction: (Saying what YOUR problem is)

Method: (Describing what you are doing about the problem.) Even though you still have your strong, powerful *self-motto*, here you will be writing your *worst* (negative) *other-motto* about the person who has bullied you and seeing what *effect* this has on everyone.

- The bully is...

How do you think your negative other-motto (your bad feelings about the bully) affects how *you* look and how *you* behave?

- How I look...

- How I behave...

How do YOU think that looking this way, and

82

behaving this way, affects how the bully now reacts to *you*?

- They now...

How does the way they now react to you make you feel about yourself? Better about yourself? Or even worse about yourself?

I feel... _____ about myself!

Results:

Did you write in how horrible they were and how much this upset you? Did you see that this made you look a certain way (perhaps angry, or scared?). And could you also see that this 'other-motto' also made a difference to the way you behaved? Perhaps you got nasty back, or perhaps you refused to go to school? Whatever you did, what was the bully's reaction to this? Did they start another fight? Did they laugh at you for not going into school? Or not even care how scared you felt? And did this just make you feel even angrier, or *more* upset?

Conclusions:

If you are anything like the other people who have done this experiment, you will have found that even your secret feelings about other people (your other-mottos) affect what happens. If your other-mottos about the bullies are all negative, this is a problem.

This is because *if we only feel bad things about people, we cannot think of good solutions to sort out the problem.* We can only think of ones like hit them or run away and that is not enough! We now understand that we need *at least* four solutions (strategies) to be successful.

Can we change the outcome (what happens)? You bet we can! Remember the pink elephant, the one I asked you NOT to *ever* remember? You know, the pink one on the wobbly blue bicycle? Yes? Then you know that we can change pretty much anything if we choose to!

Experiment number 3

Sorry, but we need to do the last experiment just once more! Write in the *Introduction* bit again first to remind yourself of exactly what is happening to you...

Introduction:

Method:

This is the really hard part but I need you to do it! Decide what GOOD things could be said about the person who has bullied you. This is called a *positive* other-motto. I need you to find at least THREE things about them! This may take a while but STICK WITH IT! First, I'm going to put in that list of positive words again to help you. But to make this experiment work, you can *only use words that you personally like*. For instance you could write that the bully is 'determined'. But if at the same time you are thinking 'determined to put me down!' that isn't positive at all! So! Just three things you would actually like about them if they weren't bullying you.

A – ambitious, amazing, adventurous

B – *bold, brave, bouncy, brilliant, beautiful*

C – creative, calm, confident, clever, considerate, caring

D – deserving, discovering, dreamy, delightful, determined

E – energetic, exciting, enthusiastic, extraordinary, excited

F – *fun, friendly, funny, fantastic, fascinating, forgiving*

G – growing, giving, good, glad, grateful, generous, gentle, giggly

H – happy, healthy, helpful, high-spirited

I – intelligent, imaginative, investigating

JK – jolly, knowledgeable, kind, keen

L – laughing, loving, learning, leader, lively, lucky, likable

M N – marvellous, modest, mysterious, natural, nice

O – optimistic, observant, organised

P – positive, peaceful, playful, persuasive, polite, praising, proud, private

Q R – quick, quiet, relaxed, responsible, reasonable, restful

S – smiling, strong, secure, sensible, sunny, successful, sociable, sympathetic, surprising

T – talented, terrific, trusting, thinking, trustworthy

UV – unique, useful, unpredictable, valuable

W, X, Y, Z – wonderful, warm, wild, wise, winning, worthwhile, Xtra-special, young, zippy

- I still may not like the bully but they are also these three good things…

- If they also are these three GOOD things, how do you think that the way you *now* feel about the bully affects how you look and how you behave?
- Because I'm remembering the good things as well, I now look...
- Because I'm remembering the good things as well, I now behave...

Because of remembering there are actually three good things, how do you think that the way you *now* look, and the way you *now* behave, might affect how the bully treats you?

When I look this new way, the bully...

And how does the better way they now react to you make you feel about yourself? Worse about yourself? Or actually *a bit better* about yourself?

- I feel... _____ about myself!

Results:

Did you write in at least three positive things about the bully? Did this new 'other-motto' change the way you looked (hopefully calmer or even friendly rather than angry or scared)? And did it also make a difference to the way you behaved? Perhaps now you felt more able to ignore the silly thing they did, or even say something to someone about helping you to sort it out?

Whatever you felt, what did you think the bully's reaction to you would be now? Did you decide it would change the way they behaved in a nice way? And did this make you feel better about yourself because now you know you can change what happens to you *for yourself*?

Conclusions:

If you are anything like all the other people who have done this experiment, you will have found that your secret feelings about other people definitely affect what happens. The good news is that you can change your secret feelings so that at least *some* of your thoughts are POSITIVE. This makes a BIG difference to what happens because if we can feel some good things about bullies, we can see there are even bits of the bully that are a little bit like us. This is a very important thing to find out because it now makes it possible to think of more solutions to sort out the bullying problem. Hooray! *And very well done!*

IMPORTANT...

You already knew that how you feel about yourself affects how others treat you.

You look friendly? People want to talk to you.

You look angry? Others avoid you!

But NOW you know that how you feel about *other people* affects how they treat you too!

Treat them like a monster? They'll behave like one! Want to stop the bullying?

I think you KNOW what I'm saying here!

And now we have the FOUR MOST IMPORTANT successful anti-bullying strategies!

1. BULLYING?

You know that if you feel bullied you have been – even if the person didn't mean it. And you know YOU have to do something about yourself fast to make you feel better!

2. STOP&THINK!

You also know that you have to be sure what you want to happen in the end because if you want other kids / teachers / parents to like you, you need to be extra careful about what you do to sort stuff out.

3. SELF-MOTTO

Remember! Most kids bully because they have found that each time they put someone else down, they feel a bit better about themselves. When they feel low, they start looking for that person who  looks easy to put down. *Now* you know that if you *feel* sad and frightened, you probably *look* sad and frightened. So you will quickly realise that the bully will see you as one of those easy targets! They put you down... and feel better. And you feel even worse. So get a store of strong, positive self-mottos ready, fast!

4. OTHER-MOTTO

You also have to remember that bullies don't just pick up on how you feel about *yourself*, they pick up on how you feel about *them* too! You NEED to remember the 1... 2... 3... good points about others as well as the bad points so that it's that much easier to sort things out and be the popular kind of person that you deserve to be!

ADULTS – CHAPTER 4

DISTRACTION / HUMOUR / FRIENDS

Technical bit:

Knowing whether you have been bullied and being able to stop and think what you need to do in order to get what you want come from having learned some *emotional* skills.

The strategies of being able to change your self-motto and your other-motto come from learning some *cognitive* (intellectual) skills.

In the next two chapters we're going to look at SIX strategies that come from learning some *social* skills.

We all spend time socialising our children. By watching us, they see what they assume is what *we* think is acceptable, appropriate behaviour. This means that if they see *us* doing something they will think that's OK and copy us. It's what children are born designed to do...

Of course, as they grow older they start copying what their friends do, or what they see on TV. For instance, one of the things that young girls see on several popular 'soaps' is that attractive girls can get what they want just by being socially manipulative. This means they do things like leaving one person out of a group, giving snide looks or making subtly unpleasant remarks in order to get their own way. It's not much better for boys. They watch older males thump / shoot / drive like lunatics and either not get hurt or be regarded as heroes! No wonder children start to think that if only they tried harder these strategies would be successful for them too!

The reason I'm giving you these next SIX strategies is because *these are the strategies that kids themselves voted as the ones that they would find really useful if they were being bullied.*

Distraction:

This is the strategy that helps you to ignore bullying. Even from here (half way up a Welsh mountain since you ask!) I can hear you yelling, "Whoa there! You told me right at the beginning that the kids you talked to said that ignoring bullies hardly *ever* works!" And you're *absolutely right* of course! This is because *when bullies have a go at you they require attention*! Sometimes they want *your* attention and sometimes they want the attention of the people they're trying to impress. Either way, if you just ignore them they're going to feel humiliated by *you*. And if *they* feel humiliated they may well feel the need to 'up the stakes' and bully you *more*.

The trick here is to ignore what the bully says *but not ignore them as a person*. Let me give you two examples:

I was in a tearing hurry to do the shopping. Deciding that what I wanted was to get out fast, I only got half of what I needed so that I could go quickly through the checkout queue for ten items or less. *The woman in front had about twenty things crammed in her basket.* What I *should* have wanted was simply to get through quickly. I could have leaned forward and nicely pointed out the ten items or less sign and asked could I please go through first, quickly? But before I gave myself time to think this through what I went for was *revenge*. What I *actually* said, none to quietly, and to anyone behind her back who would listen, "I *thought* this queue was for only *ten* items!"

Now that I'd put *her* down, the woman in front wanted to humiliate *me* too! She turned round and made some very loud and very personal remarks about my age, my social standing and my education (something along the lines of 'Interfering, middle-class old idiot')! I stuck my nose in the air and looked the other way. She tried even louder remarks about my lack of human kindness and understanding. I *still* pretended to ignore her. She lost all patience and now banged her umbrella sharply on my basket... Suddenly she definitely had my *full* attention! I looked wildly at the checkout assistant for help. The checkout assistant looked equally wildly the other way! I now realised with blinding clarity that what I *really* wanted, more than anything, was to escape from this encounter with all my body parts intact!

Despite my panic I remembered a different, really useful strategy. One adults use all the time with demanding children. The one I'd discussed at length with all the kids I'd worked with. I used the distraction strategy on her. I took a deep breath, completely ignored *what she had said* (and even the umbrella prodding!) and asked her politely if it was still raining outside. I have to say she looked at me as if I was completely insane for a moment, but she gathered herself together and replied conversationally that it certainly had been when she came into the store. The checkout assistant hurriedly checked out her basket and I waited my turn!

So, to repeat, if you ignore bullies, they will only try harder to gain your attention. In this case initially I had bullied her by talking behind her back about her ignoring the sign (my fault). When she took offence at this I ended up feeling bullied too. Of course we *could* have ended up throwing our supermarket baskets on the floor and having an all out fight! This was NOT what I wanted to happen! But by distracting her by talking about something completely different I gave her the attention she now needed but not at my expense. What about just waiting in the longer queue? Even though I knew that this would have saved me having to use the distraction strategy I still felt pleased with myself. I got out of a really difficult situation in a way that meant we all (me, the lady with 20 items *and* the checkout assistant) felt reasonably OK about ourselves in the end!

Can children use this strategy successfully? I was once asked into a school to help a very sweet, bespectacled ten-year-old called Katy. Katy's teacher was aware that this little girl was becoming withdrawn at school and this teacher had a feeling that somewhere along the line Katy was being bullied. She just couldn't get Katy to say *how*. She *seemed* fine with her friends at school but she had lost her confidence and wasn't doing so well at her schoolwork. The teacher told me that Katy's parents were also very worried but that they too couldn't get her to say what the problem was.

I chatted to Katy about her friends, I asked her whether she thought bullying went on in her class. She said not really. I asked her if bullying went on *outside* her class. She hung her head and agreed that she *thought* it might go on but it wasn't a big thing. "What kind of not-a-big-thing?" I asked her. She burst into tears. Apparently, on the way to school each day a gang of girls from a nearby school often made silly remarks like, "Hello, *four* eyes!" and then dissolved into gales of laughter. Katy wanted to know, "Is this bullying?" And is it? If you and I are still agreed that anything that makes you feel humiliated and small (whether intended or not) is bullying, Katy was definitely being bullied. I told her she was right to feel upset and I was sorry that these girls had been horrid to her. I suggested that now we knew it *was* bullying we should spend some time sorting it out in a way that made her feel good about herself again and she agreed to do this.

I asked Katy what she wanted to happen. She wasn't sure so we tried a few possibilities. For instance, did she want revenge? Someone to shout back at these girls or an adult to report them to their own school? She thought about this for about one second. "If they get into trouble (she meant if someone humiliates *them*) they'll just get more horrible to me when they see me!" she said. "What I really want is for them to stop being nasty to me. Just to say 'Hello' without being rude." Brilliant! Once she knew what positive outcome she wanted we could work on how to achieve this for her.

We worked on Katy's self-motto. Instead of her timid, "I'm not good at standing up for myself and I look stupid with glasses," she came up with, "I'm smiley and I've got lots of friends at my school and I think I look quite nice." Which was a *huge* step forward.

We also worked on Katy's *other*-motto for these girls. Initially it was simply "They are horrible, I hate them!" But eventually (it took a *long* time and was a bit like pulling teeth!) Katy came up with, "One of them looks a bit friendlier than the others and if they were my friends I would think they were quite fashionable." We now had something to work with. Instead of facing these girls the next day looking anxious and ready to burst into tears, Katy was ready with a confident facial expression and body language (her positive self-motto). And she was able to see that there were at least *some* good points about these girls who had made her feel so miserable (her positive other-motto).

We had also practised together how she might use the distraction strategy. The next day, walking to school, the other girls saw her but said nothing. But on the second day they shouted, "It's the four-eyed freaky girl!" just as they were passing her. As she and I had practised, Katy was ready for them. She breathed deeply… and asked them if they had the time because her watch had broken! This was really brave of her and I congratulated her on this. Then I asked her, "How did they react to being asked?" Katy was ecstatic! She said they had just looked at their watches and told her it was 8:15! One of them had even asked her if she was late? She had said no, she was just in time, and thank you.

These girls have never bothered Katy since. But then, she has never looked like an easy target since. Her appearance *has* changed, but she hasn't changed her specs. She just reminds herself of the things she likes about herself and remembers that if you don't ignore people, but treat them as if they're OK, they're likely to respond well. *They* just want attention. *You* choose whether to make that attention positive or negative.

It's a life skill that will stand Katy in good stead when she starts at secondary school in the Autumn.

Humour (what is funny and what is definitely not):
Despite every birth control method known to man
(and woman), my partner and I unexpectedly gained
one bright, adorable, and beautiful daughter. We even
eventually decided that we would like another one.
We abandoned birth control. But nothing happened.
My family (who know me well and *would not dare* ask)
wisely said nothing. My husband's family, however,
were not so cautious… "*Still* no more babies?" nagged
one auntie every single time we saw her. Noting my
teeth clamped ever more firmly together, another
relative suggested we try the following phrase, "Not
yet Auntie! But tonight we are going to try again
especially for you!" My husband and I rocked with
laughter. But when we tried this phrase on the
aforementioned auntie, she was less than amused. She
took to telling everyone how *over-sensitive* we were at
family gatherings. And we felt increasingly
humiliated and isolated.

And this is the difficulty with using humour to
defuse bullying. If it veers even ever so slightly into
sarcasm, it will make the bully feel threatened! They
may well now decide to be even *more* unpleasant. If
the bullying is happening to you, you might be
prepared to risk this happening. If it's happening to
your child, only they can decide whether it's worth it
– you cannot risk doing it on their behalf.

So what kind of humour *is* funny? I'm going to put
this in capital letters because it's so important! ONLY
HUMOUR DIRECTED AT YOURSELF! Interviews

with successful comics show a common thread. Most of them became comics because they found this was a successful way to deal with those who bullied them when they were at school. And did they get their own back by making these bullies look like idiots? No, they did not. They learned to deflect the bully's comments by making jokes *at their own expense*. The term that describes this kind of humour (self-effacing) might not initially sound as if it's much fun. But as an anti-bullying strategy it is *immensely* successful. You don't have to *continually* put yourself down – just once or twice usually makes the point...

And whilst we're on the subject, I have heard people say that surely being funny is something you're either born with or not. I have to admit that some people are better at it than others, but I still stand by my conviction that anyone can *learn* to lighten up a bit. It's just a social skill like any other. After all, we have to *learn* to be polite. We could equally easily learn not to take ourselves too seriously!

Could Katy have used humour as a strategy? Supposing she and the gang of bullies all go on to attend the same secondary school? Suppose they pick on her straight away on the first day "Hello, four-eyes! We remember *you*!" If Katy quips back "I remember *you* too, two-eyes!" they might laugh. On the other hand, they might just as easily get nastier because they suspect she's being sarcastic. This is a real problem. Humour depends on several things. Such as who's *telling* the joke. And who they're telling it *t o*. And also on whether you share a particular sense of humour!

This makes using humour as a strategy a really, really difficult thing to do. In all our experiments with it, the kids I worked with found that sometimes it went absolutely*brilliantly* and defused the difficult situation really successfully. Suddenly people thought you were great and you had more friends! And I have to be honest with you here – sometimes it went horribly wrong! Others thought they were being sarcastic and rude and things got worse instead of better!

So why have I included humour as a strategy? I've done it because kids say they like it and they know that when they get it right it's fantastic. But they also agreed with me that it's risky and needs practice. But bear in mind that even if you aren't quite getting it right, being able to smile at yourself is still another *great* way of raising your self-esteem so you're *still* winning!

Incidentally, just in case there's any interest out there, my husband and I eventually decided to stick with having just one child and I would start a career once she began school. Fired with ambition, and to be absolutely sure of no 'surprises', we returned to using birth control. And then, you guessed it… within three months I was pregnant with bright, adorable, and beautiful daughter number two.

Friends:

You don't really need me to spell this strategy out, do you? We all need friends of one sort or another. But what if we feel we (as a good parent) are already providing the perfect friend for our child? Sorry, it's not enough! There's plenty of scientific evidence to show that having a few, good friends outside the family circle can make all the difference between depression and happiness. Sometimes we have almost perfect friends who nearly always do and say the right things. But mostly our friends have different functions – we go shopping with one, to the cinema with another, etc. I talk to one friend about work problems and with another we laugh about life until we cry. The important thing is that being able to talk in depth with our friends means we don't feel isolated. Not feeling isolated means we are less likely to get depressed. And the same goes for our children. They too need a range of friends. We can steer them in the right direction by our example, and we can also be welcoming to their choice of friend.

Take the case of Katy. She had told no one of her problems and had been feeling very miserable. She and I discussed how it might be useful to talk through what had happened with her friends. Even though she hadn't expected anything to come of this, what she found was that once she had, she suddenly felt less isolated emotionally. She also found that several of them were happy to walk with her to school.

However, one day she may well end up at the same school as the girls who currently bully her. And she may even become friendly with them. Despite what has happened, how do you feel Katy's parents will feel about this? We would all understand it if they found it hard. But if they really care about Katy developing into a strong, individual adult who will cope with life when they are not there to protect her, they will swallow their pride and accept these girls for whatever qualities Katy finds valuable in them!

And yes, I *do* know that this is not always easy! As a teenager, bright, adorable, and beautiful daughter number two (now supporting a shaven head – except for five blue plaits over her forehead) had friends who arrived clad entirely in black, and reeking of cigarettes. Not only was it hard to distinguish one of these friends from another, we could never understand what they were actually saying. "Usberther?" they snarled on the doorstep. We screwed up our eyes in concentration, mimed old age and deafness, and asked, *"Sorry?"* "USBERTHER?" they growled back menacingly. Eventually of course we understood that this meant "Is Beatrice there?" and we were able to respond, a tad anxiously, that yes, she was indeed there and invite them in!

The point of telling you this is that eventually we grew to thoroughly enjoy the visits of these friends. It has given us huge pleasure over the years to watch them grow into the lovely young adults they now are, complete with academic degrees, mortgages, and children of their own! Although we certainly *didn't* think we'd like them to start with, being determined to get on with your children's friends can repay you many times over.

So now you have SEVEN positive anti-bullying strategies to help your child stop the bullying that's happening to them!

1. BULLYING? Is it *teasing* or bullying? It doesn't matter which you call it – if it makes us feel wretched it needs sorting out.

2. STOP&THINK! What do you want to be the *outcome* of this sorting out? Do you want to score points? Or do you want to achieve something positive for your child?

3. SELF-MOTTO Changing a negative self-motto to a positive one raises self-esteem. It not only changes the way we *feel* about ourselves – this feeling changes our body language – which will change the way other people treat us too.

4. OTHER-MOTTO Changing the way you feel about others to include positive things *also* raises our self-esteem. It reminds us that we have the power to change how we feel about others. And that feeling more positive about others makes it easier to sort out that bullying – which is what we want.

5. DISTRACTION This is the strategy you use when you need to ignore the horrible thing someone did or said but not ignore them. It doesn't mean you agree with them, it just means you choose to distract them rather than try to deal with it – because you recognise that the alternative is a no-win situation.

6. HUMOUR Sarcasm makes aggressive situations even worse – only being able to laugh at yourself every now and then makes the situation easier.
7. FRIENDS You need them, I need them, your children need them. Their choice may not be yours and you may need to use your other-motto strategy at first until you get to understand what it is about them that your child values.

What's in it for you?

List the bullying behaviours and situations that make life for your family stressful. Work out, on a scale of one-to-ten, how stressful each one of those things is. Starting with the EASIEST one on your list, use all the strategies you've learnt so far to sort it out. Now re-check it on your scale of one-to-ten and see what happens. Congratulations!

Kids - Chapter 4

If you've done all the exercises and experiments in the first three chapters you will have the FOUR most important strategies. Without

those strategies firmly under your belt, the last SIX strategies are not so easy to do. So please, please PROMISE me that whatever else you do, you will practise and practise the *BULLYING?* /

STOP&THINK! / *SELF-MOTTO* / *OTHER-MOTTO* strategies over and over – until you can do them almost without thinking, every time something upsets you!

Strategy 5: Distraction

How often have you been told to ignore bullies and then they'll stop? This is something that a lot of grown-ups suggest because they have found it useful. The trouble is, it's only useful if you have lots of other strategies up your sleeve – or if you are powerful enough to stop bullies in other ways from doing too much damage. At your age you may not feel you have much power. And you definitely don't have much power if the bully is bigger or stronger or more popular than you!

Although they *seem* to feel good about themselves, the kids who bully are the ones who used *not* to feel good about themselves. Kids who bully have found (using their own experiments) that when they say mean things to other kids (to make those kids feel small) it makes them feel bigger and more powerful for a bit. BUT IT ONLY MAKES THEM FEEL MORE POWERFUL IF THE KID THEY PICK ON HAS A BIG REACTION! For instance the kid being picked on might cry, or shout back, or run away. And this is why grown-ups say to ignore it because grown-ups know one of the reasons the bully picks on YOU is that you give a particular reaction that the bully enjoys – you might need to think about what it is…

Anyway, there is a big problem with ignoring bullies and FIFTEEN more gold stars if you have worked out what it is! It's this:

If you just ignore the bully, they will keep on being nasty to you until you DO cry / shout / run away.

So what you need is a strategy that means that bullies get the attention they need from you but in a good way that doesn't make you look stupid! This means we need to *distract* them…

Exercise:

We want to see whether what you say back to the bully makes any difference to what happens. Ask your parent or your best friend to practise this exercise with you. Imagine you are both in a classroom, waiting for the teacher to arrive...

Parent or best friend (you have to pretend to be the bully):
- Say something untrue and mean like "Why is your hair orange like a carrot? Are your parents carrots then?"

You:
- You have ten seconds to pretend to cry or shout back! Go for it!

Parent or best friend:
- If you were a real bully, how do you think you would have responded to all that crying or shouting? Now you have the whole class's attention, wouldn't you just laugh and feel 'mission accomplished'?
- What about the teacher when they arrive? Might they not just feel fed-up that no one is getting ready for the lesson they spent all yesterday evening preparing and dish out detentions to *everyone* even if it was only the bully's fault?

You:
- Tell me, now the bully is laughing at you and you have a detention, do you feel better about yourself, or *worse*?

SWAP PLACES! This time *you* be the bully and upset your friend or parent. See how it feels when they get upset and make a fuss. Does it make *you* feel quite powerful for a few minutes? Well now you know why bullies do it! The huge problem for them is that this will only make them feel good for those few minutes. What you need to learn (and show them) is a way that gets attention but in a way that helps everyone to feel fine.

Try the exercise again! We'll go for the new approach here so that the bullying stops.

Parent or best friend:
• Make another mean comment intended to make your child / best friend feel stupid.

You:
• STOP and take a DEEP BREATH.
• *Remember that the main thing you want is for the bully to stop bullying you.*
• Think of something *completely different* to say like, "What are we having for breakfast today?"

Parent or best friend:
Well, what *are* you having?

You:
• Now how do you feel? *You have stopped the bullying!* Do you feel better or worse? I know, it's a daft question! Seriously though, WELL DONE! Keep practising this strategy so that you can do it without a minute's thought! You have now learnt that even if you can't deal with what someone *says*

you can STILL cope. You just give the bully the attention they need and you still come out of it looking cool!

Strategy 6 – Humour
(Knowing what's funny and what's not!)

What makes me laugh and what makes you laugh can be very different! For instance, little children fall over laughing when they say things like "Bottom" and "Poo" and "Wee-wee". Call me old and boring, but I can't for the life of me roll on the floor laughing about this!

So when grown-ups say things like "You could try being funny when you get teased", it can be a bit of a minefield. For instance, suppose someone calls you fat. What if you say "Not as fat as you! You're fatter than a fat pig with a wig on!" I mean, that's quite funny isn't it? But will it get you what you want (stop the bullying and make you look good at the same time)? No, it probably will not. And it will make the bully a whole lot crosser! Now you have an *angry* fat pig with a wig on...

What stops bullying – and makes you look good – is when you are able to laugh at YOURSELF. This is hard to do when you feel you are already being put down, but trust me, it works. Next time some kid says, "Why do you wear dorky trainers?" try saying, "You think these are dorky? You should see what my mum *wanted* to buy me!" You'll have them thinking you're

OK in no time because they can see you can laugh at yourself (so they don't need to put you down).

What are you waiting for? You know the drill! Go and practise this strategy too and see how well it works! The important thing to remember here is that sarcasm (putting somebody *else* down) will make things *worse*. And that isn't what we're aiming to do at all, is it? To be a positive, successful strategy it has to end up with everyone feeling BETTER about themselves!

Strategy 7 – Friends (and why you need them)

Don't ask me why, it's just one of those horrible facts about the human race. If you are seen as not having friends at school, not only will you feel a bit left out, you will also be more likely to get picked on by other kids.

You would think, wouldn't you, that after all these years of so-called civilization, people could be nicer than that. But no, like lions looking for a little zebra by a water hole with thousands of big zebra, bullies look for the easiest target in a whole classroom of students.

So can I make a suggestion here? If you get bullied and are often on your own, join a group. Usually there are after-school groups like swimming or guides / scouts that you could join. Set yourself the target of talking to one new person every week. It can seem scary at first but you're all interested in the same thing, so that makes it easier to say something about what you're all doing. Practise different things to say at home with your family, your dog or even saying it to yourself in the mirror! Eventually, if you give it 100%, you'll find that learning this new skill of joining in with others will make you feel better about yourself. The important thing is building up a group of people you can talk to / do things with.

Once you've got the hang of talking with others who are all interested in the same things as you, it's only a short step to finding it easier to talk to kids in your class at school as well. Find out what interests them, ask questions about their interests, listen to their answers. Keep practising it until you can do it well. Easy!

But what if you *have* friends and it is actually one of your friends who is bullying you? This can be really, really painful and I'm very sorry if this is happening to you. But believe me, it *often* happens this way with groups of friends. It happens because we don't all feel good about ourselves all of the time. So sometimes it will be one person putting other kids in the group down (so that this person feels better about themselves for a bit) and sometimes it is another kid doing it. Now that you know this (kids put others down so that they feel better about themselves) you are in a very powerful position. Why? Because you understand what is going on! I'm going to put the next bit in capital letters because it is so important:

BULLYING IS NOT ABOUT *YOU* NOT BEING GOOD ENOUGH. IT IS ABOUT OTHERS FEELING *THEY'RE* NOT GOOD ENOUGH! So now you know.

And showing that you understand and can accept this is a big step forward to having lots of friends who really like you.

So! Where have we got to now? You have SEVEN strategies! You have now learnt:

1. BULLYING?

You know that if you *feel* bullied you have been – even if the person didn't mean to bully you and even if it was only once. And you know you have to do something about yourself fast to make you feel better!

2. STOP&THINK!

You also know that you have to be sure what you want to happen in the end because if you want other kids / the bully / teachers / parents to like you, you need to be extra careful about what you do to sort stuff out.

3. SELF-MOTTO

Remember! Most kids bully because they have found that each time they put someone else down, they feel a bit better about themselves. When they feel low, they start looking for that person who looks easy to put down. *Now* you know that if you *feel* sad and frightened, you probably *look* sad and frightened. So you will quickly realise that the bully will see you as one of those easy targets! They put you down… and feel better. And you feel even worse. So get a store of strong, positive self-mottos ready, fast!

4. OTHER-MOTTO

You also have to remember that bullies don't just pick up on how you feel about *yourself*, they pick up on how you feel about *them* too! You NEED to remember the 1... 2... 3... good points about others as well as the bad points so that it's that much easier to sort things out and be the popular kind of person that you deserve to be!

5. DISTRACTION

This means that although you can't ignore the actual bully (because they need your attention so badly they are prepared to be nasty in order to get it), you can choose to ignore what they actually said or did because you can't deal with that right now. The trick here is to distract them from what they said by talking about something completely different.

6. HUMOUR

Judging what other people find funny is a risky thing! They *might* think you are very, very witty and want to be your friend forever. Or they might think you are being sarcastic and rude! Being able to tell a joke against yourself every now and then is fine. Just don't do it too often – the important thing is for you to feel good about yourself and your ability to handle bullies, not put yourself down all the time.

7. FRIENDS

Not only are you less likely to be picked on when you're with friends, you will also have people to talk to about any bullying that's happened and how you want to sort it out. Learning to make friends is a skill you can learn like any other skill. You find out how to do it and you practise and practise and practise until you can do it!

IMPORTANT...

You are very nearly a STRATEGY STAR! You should be feeling pretty good about yourself by now!

ADULTS – CHAPTER 5

APPEARANCE, FLATTERY AND REWARDS

It doesn't seem possible that we are already on to the last THREE strategies. But here we are… These are the last three strategies that children and teenagers said they would most like to be able to use if they were being bullied. I've described them for you and given you examples as before. And then, just so you don't get bored, in the next chapter I've also given you some practise!

Appearance:
Families are very individual. This is good news – diversity is important in the human race. You may be a family who is very careful about their appearance. Or in your family it may not matter how you look. One of the things that matters in bullying is how different your child looks from what is considered normal by the bullies in their class. Bullies are not good at understanding that others can be different from them. If *your* child is considered different in

some way, you have two choices. You can let them sink or you can teach them to swim. If you choose to help them swim (you *m u s t*!) your children will have to work extra hard on their self-motto and their social skills, so that the great person they indubitably are can shine through the bully's narrow ideas on what / who is acceptable.

Anyone reading this book who has a child with a medical condition that makes them look in any way different will know all of this with blinding clarity. Right from the birth of your baby you will have had to cope with not only your own feelings about your child looking different from how you had expected, but with the feelings of your friends and family too. Parents of this group of children already know how important appearance is to a child trying to fit in with their group. Research shows that the *most* important thing about starting school, aged five, is that *children feel confident about the way they look.* Please note the emphasis in that sentence. It does not say that five-year-olds have to look great, it says they have to feel confident about the way they look. At five, a lot of a child's confidence (their self-motto) will have been encouraged by supportive family members like you.

Can I make another point here about appearance? What if your child dresses the same, and has nothing different about them except that they are particularly *attractive?* Surely no one is going to bully *them* because of the way they look? If you have such a child and that child is being bullied, you will know this is not true. There is a theory that is called 'the just world theory'. This theory explains how some people think that life should somehow be balanced out. You know the stuff – if you're rich you probably aren't happy. If you're beautiful you're probably shallow. That sort of thing. You can see that the kind of child who justifies all the bad things that happen to them by thinking that *life should be fair* is likely to believe in this 'just world' theory. Armed with this, the child who gains their self-esteem by putting others down may feel perfectly justified in doing this to a child who is more attractive than them – just to even out the odds! So if your child is average in every way *except* they are beautiful, I'm afraid they too will have to work particularly hard on their self-motto and their social skills. And whilst we're on the subject, might this apply to children who are unusually clever? What do *you* think!

Rebecca, an outsider in her class, was often picked on. She was a pretty girl but dressed very differently from the rest of her class. Regardless of what other children in her class wore, Rebecca's mum, Phillipa, was strongly of the opinion that what we wear is not important. Moreover, however much Rebecca tried to convince her mum, there was *no way* this mum was going to let her daughter choose her own clothes or buy anything she thought was unsuitable. Phillipa's main argument was that fashion is expensive and a waste of money.

It took an hour of explaining to Rebecca's mum that even though fashion *can* be a waste of money and world resources, for children and teenagers *fitting in with their group is vitally important*. They find their general appearance an endless source of difficulty. Their emerging hormones often mean spots and lank hair. Added to this, they grow asymmetrically. This means that they don't just grow bigger – different parts of them grow at different times! So hands and feet grow first followed by arms and legs and finally body! No *wonder* they go through clumsy stages! And they all do this at different times so that in one class of thirteen-year-olds you will have some that look about seven and others who look about twenty! Phillipa was beginning to understand why teenagers feel the need to conform...

Rebecca's desire to dress like her friends wasn't particularly about fashion. It was about that fitting in with her group that young people have a basic need to do. Once Phillipa had understood this she was great. Straight off she and Rebecca arranged a compromise. Phillipa stated an amount that could be spent on clothes each term and *within reason* Rebecca chose them. The within reason clause was because Phillipa quite rightly insisted on certain things like shoes that looked good but would also keep her feet dry! But she was totally prepared for Rebecca to choose the one expensive black 'designer' T-shirt that *she* wanted instead of the four cheaper ones in jolly colours that Phillipa would have preferred.

Rebecca feels more confident now that she fits in more with her classmates. And this confidence has helped her to make friends. Result! What's more, Phillipa also understands that the more confident Rebecca feels about the way she *looks*, the more confident she feels about herself *as a person*. Phillipa is a terrific mum. She certainly didn't need me to explain what she already knows – that Rebecca also needs to understand that popularity depends on working on her social skills as much as on her appearance. This is a fantastic gift for a mother to give her daughter.

Flattery (but it's got to be genuine):

I don't want to bore you rigid with stories of my life but I must come clean and admit that one of the reasons I'm so interested in bullying is that I myself have been *very* bad at dealing with it over the years. And I'm *particularly* grateful to have found ways of coping with it in my old age! Anyway, to explain to you why flattery has to be genuine, I'll tell you about the first house my husband and I ever bought. It was in a district that had just escaped demolition. Houses were really cheap and full of what house improvement programmes like to call 'period features'. Young families like us flocked into the area and snapped up bargains. When we arrived at *our* period feature packed bargain we had neighbours we never saw. We assumed they were nurses doing various shifts because there seemed to be a lot of to-ing and fro-ing at night. It was weeks before my husband was propositioned by one of these neighbours on his way home from work ("Ah, how kind but no thank you" he replied. Ever the gentleman). Finally we realised we had bought a house next door to a brothel.

The point I'm slowly drawing you towards depends on telling you about the day I was returning from the tax office. We were being wildly over-taxed. Phone calls / letters to the tax office were ignored. So despite torrential rain, incipient bubonic plague and a tired two-year-old, I went personally to the tax office. They patiently explained that the tax was based on my husband's salary. I asked to see the figures. They were happy to show me. Every month he had been paid (if I can still remember) £620.40. Well, every month bar April when their figures showed him as earning £6,204 "He is a school teacher," I pointed out. "School teachers do not earn £6,204 a month" (this was 1974). "Ah, no," they obligingly agreed, "Our mistake! We'll put a cheque in the post." Mission accomplished.

So I staggered home (wailing two-year-old warm and dry inside pushchair, me soaked and frozen outside). Beyond all caring and wiping a streaming nose on my (spectacularly unflattering) old duffel coat sleeve I trudged up our road. As I approached our gate, I glowered ferociously at a man standing outside the brothel next door. Startled – even, possibly, terrified – he used the flattery strategy in the face of my rage, "Well hallo there, sexy!" he cried nervously, "What about a jump?"

The point is, leaving out the bits about being

mistaken for a prostitute, was I flattered that this man said I looked sexy? Gentle reader, not only was I *not* flattered, I gathered strength from my increased rage and, despite the wailing pushchair occupant, chased this stranger down the road shrieking, like a banshee, "How *dare* you call me sexy!"

One way to defuse aggression is undoubtedly to give the person that you find scary a genuine compliment. It not only takes the wind out of their sails, it also gives them the attention they crave – but in a positive way. *Just learn from the experience above that the flattery needs to be sincere and it needs to be welcome!*

James, a lively and likable young lad, had just started at a new school. He longed to be part of a particular gang of lads who played football at lunch breaks. He hung around at the edges of this group but they consistently ignored him. He could see no way of ever even talking to them. By the time I met him he was in despair! He was clear that he was *not* actually being bullied but that *being ignored felt a bit like being bullied*. I asked him if he'd ever asked straight out if he could join in and he said that was too difficult in case they said no!

So we knew that James wasn't really being bullied but felt miserable all the same. We also knew what he wanted to happen (he wanted to play football with them)! We did a quick session on James's self-motto so that he felt a bit more confident about himself. Instead of feeling he 'might not be good enough to play' he decided to feel that 'he was good enough to have a go'.

We also had a look at his other-motto for the group of boys and he realised that it had become "They're too stuck up to let me play!" We had to change that fast and he came up with "They just haven't really noticed me yet!"

I then suggested to James that a compliment might also go down well here. After all, boys who spend a lot of time playing football are often happy to have others mention how well they do it! We briefly practised how James could do this. And he went straight out and did it! He saw two of the boys at break and mentioned that he'd watched them play and he was really impressed. It would be nice to hear that they instantly said "Thank you. Please join our team!" They didn't. But they *did* speak to him when they saw him on future occasions and a few weeks later he felt bold enough to ask right out if he could join in and play. They said yes. Job done!

Rewards:

Do you ever have a really, really hard day and at the end of it sit slumped in front of the TV with a giant bar of chocolate and / or a bottle of wine saying, "I *deserve* this!" as if it was a treat? Do you say it even though you know what your *body* would regard as a treat is a square meal and a walk? Do you *still* say it the day after when you feel bloated and hung-over? Why, when we feel over-stressed, do we find it so hard to treat ourselves to, say, an early night?

I once worked with a family that was having

increasing problems with 'rewards'. They claimed that not only was bullying emotionally distressing, it was financially distressing too! I asked them what they meant by this. Alan, the dad, explained that they had removed their son Andrew (aged twelve) from the large, local comprehensive where he had been badly bullied by 'a bunch of thugs'. Even though the family couldn't really afford it, they had placed Andrew in a small, select private school. Alan explained that he himself had been bullied at school as a child – he was determined that this shouldn't happen to Andrew. And for a time Andrew seemed so much happier. Whatever the sacrifices, the move seemed worth it and Alan felt it had been a good decision to move his son.

However, Andrew now came home from school anxious about not being able to go on all the school trips that better-off families were able to afford for their children. Alan felt inadequate for not being able to send Andrew and Andrew in turn grew ever more insistent and demanding. He now felt that he *deserved* those rewards. Alan began to wonder if his once distressed and timid son, Andrew, was now bullying *him*! Every time Alan provided yet another thing that Andrew demanded, Alan felt more resentful and Andrew grew more convinced that he was entitled to everything he wanted to compensate for any bad things he had endured! Andrew's parents were confused. They had made a difficult and expensive decision, but knowing their son was safe was their reward and they had hoped it would be Andrew's reward too. They spent hours and hours endlessly discussing (arguing?) where they might have gone wrong but were unable to think of an alternative.

So what *had* gone wrong? I asked Alan and Andrew if they would be prepared to go through all the strategies with me. Alan didn't exactly refuse, but he made it clear that the problem was his son's recent attitude rather than a problem within the family dynamics. He made it clear that he felt understandably threatened that I might be suggesting he hadn't already done his best. I replied that I thought he had done what many parents do – he had, at enormous cost to himself, leapt like a knight in shining armour onto his horse and rescued his son. I agreed that given their circumstances I would have been very tempted to do exactly the same thing. And I too would have felt that saving my child was my reward. However, one of the things that teenagers made very clear to me when I worked with them was that *they do not want to be rescued*. Initially, what they want is help to sort things out for themselves. Only when they themselves recognise that despite all their efforts this is not working do they want adults to interfere. Nor do they regard being rescued as a reward. They often just see it as a sign that they themselves have failed.

So Alan had to be a hero a second time. This time he and Andrew went through all the strategies together. They agreed absolutely on the Bullying?

strategy – Andrew had been bullied. But they quickly came unstuck on the Stop & Think! strategy. Andrew admitted to his dad that he had felt even more of a failure moving schools because he knew he still didn't know how to stop bullying for himself. He even, finally, admitted that he had resented his father making the decision without consulting him. Alan was dismayed that Andrew felt this way and it was obvious that they were now both upset. I suggested that the only way out of this was to move forward. They needed to learn the rest of the strategies so that in future they would be able to use them as a point of reference to sort out any future difficulties.

So over the next couple of weeks we worked on Self-Motto and Other Motto. Alan saw a side of his son that he hadn't seen before – instead of a dependent, demanding boy he recognised him as someone who wanted the power to make mistakes, take the consequences, and grow into an independent adult. Alan then watched his son practise his social skills so that he could hold his own at the new school without the need for the expensive extras. He was impressed! In fact, Alan was so impressed that he began to revise the way he himself coped at work. He admitted that his staff had found him a bit of a tyrant because he retained all control in his business. Once he felt good about himself (he had his own strong, confident self-motto) he was more relaxed. Once he was able to see the good points in his workforce (he gave them more positive other-mottos than of old) he was able to relax his grip on every detail. He too practised his social skills. His staff found him more approachable. Alan began to see the world as a less threatening place. And because he is Andrew's role model, Andrew found it easier to do the same.

And their reward for all this effort? Andrew chose basketball (and his mother nearly became demented listening to the ball bang against the side of the house every evening!). Alan chose to take his wife out one evening a week to talk about anything other than Andrew's problems! And I got quite tearful thinking what a thoroughly nice family they were.

So! You too now have TEN successful, positive anti-bullying strategies!

1. BULLYING? Is it *teasing* or bullying? It doesn't matter which you call it – if it makes you feel wretched it needs sorting out.
2. STOP&THINK! What do you want to be the *outcome* of this sorting out? Do you want to score points? Or do you want to achieve something positive for your child?
3. SELF-MOTTO Changing a negative self-motto to a positive one raises self-esteem. It not only changes the way you *feel* about yourself – this feeling changes your body language and this will change the way other people treat you too.
4. OTHER-MOTTO Changing the way you feel about others to include positive things *also* raises your

self-esteem. It reminds you that you have the power to change how you feel about others. And that feeling more positive about others makes it easier to sort out that bullying – which is what you want.

5. DISTRACTION This is the strategy you use when you need to ignore the horrible thing someone did or said but not ignore them. It doesn't mean you agree with them, it just means you choose to distract them rather than try to deal with it – because you recognise that the alternative is a no-win situation.

6. HUMOUR Sarcasm makes aggressive situations even worse – only being able to laugh at yourself every now and then makes the situation easier.

7. FRIENDS You need them, I need them, your children need them. Their choice may not be yours and you may need to use your other-motto strategy at first until you get to understand what it is about them that your child values.

8. APPEARANCE It's a developmental thing with kids – they need to know where they fit in. One of the ways they do this is through wearing similar clothes. Helping them to do this in a way that still recognises that eventually it will be their *personality* that matters is a brilliant way of showing them that you understand.

9. FLATTERY People generally love a sincere compliment. And if you've been careful to

compliment them on something *they* care about, they are likely to think more highly of you!

10. REWARD Bullying is about negative energy and power. Sorting out bullying in a positive way is about summoning up energy for positive personal power – and this can be exhausting. Give yourself a positive reward for all that fantastic, positive effort!

What's in it for you?

If you continually rescue your child you disempower them. As children grow older and desperate for the confidence they need to live without their parents, the healthy ones will begin to resent all that rescuing. The scary thing is that many will take their revenge by bullying their protective parents... What you have to consider is, 'Can we afford, emotionally or financially, to send our bullying children off to 'Brat Camp' in Utah? Or would it be easier to just get on and teach them the life skills they still need – and we now have?'

Kids - Chapter 5

Seven successful anti-bullying strategies down! Only THREE more to go!

Appearance (Yes, it does matter!)

One of the really irritating things about being a kid is that when you get really worried about your spots / what you're going to wear, adults always tell you that the way you look doesn't matter! "Don't worry!" they say, "no one will notice!" It makes you want to scream, doesn't it? And it's even more irritating when they expect you to wear something you don't even like because they want you to look a certain way for church or great grandmother's birthday party!

Well I'm going to say right here that I think how you look IS really important. And I think adults are not being very honest with children if they say that no one notices. How often do you see *them* going out to work in their pyjamas, for instance? Or going to the shops in a swim suit? Not very often? No! And that's because mostly they care about how they look! You won't see *them* going to parties in the same thing they've worn all day (like school uniform), no sir! They know that other people are going to make a snap decision about them based just on seeing them. You already know this too. Doing something about it can be a bit harder.

So what *do* you do if you have very little choice about what you are allowed to wear? You may need to wear certain clothes because of your religion. This doesn't mean you can't still be stylish. For example – I have a Muslim friend who would not dream of going out without covering her hair. Although not all Muslim women are this strict, my friend feels that covering her hair in public is important. I asked her if she had always minded this rule. She said she had when she was a teenager so she had taken particular care to have her hair looking beautiful under her scarf! Why does this matter when no one could see it? It matters because it made her feel more confident!

Of course, some people feel they don't have much choice about their appearance because they have a disfigurement or disability. It can be hard finding fashionable clothes if you're not a standard size or shape. Putting in the effort because you know you're worth it will make you feel good about yourself (it will raise your self-esteem). I know how this feels too. Ages ago I lost an eye. And no, this doesn't mean I went to the park one day, took an eye out to look at it and then dropped it! It was just that one eye had cancer in it and had to be removed. I have a plastic eye instead and even if you look hard it's pretty hard to tell which one it is most days. Except those days when I have to do a TV interview. Now you may think it's pretty exciting to be on TV, but trust me, when you don't feel confident about the way you look it's a nightmare. And when those huge camera lights shine on my plastic eye it looks... well it looks *plastic*. And knowing this makes me anxious and I forget what I want to say. The good news is that one of my daughters found me a fantastic eye patch! Now I can concentrate on what I want to say instead of fussing about how I want to look!

Of course, what we're talking about here is just looking your best. It's not about designer labels and it doesn't need to cost a fortune. But some people DO spend a huge amount on looking good. They even have surgery (which can mean hospital surgeons cutting skin, breaking bones and putting plastic bits into bodies). Only you will be able to decide whether you want this sort of thing as an adult. But for now, just try looking the best you can. Things like keeping clean and caring for your hair and teeth! If you have a battle with your parents over clothes, see if you can reach a compromise. They choose your shoes, you choose your jeans and T-shirts. Then check that you have learnt all the anti-bullying strategies really well. You are extra confident about who you are and don't need to go to extremes.

Flattery (Saying something nice!)

One of the scariest things about school is the fact that there are times and places when the teachers never seem to be around. Things like long corridors when you are going to the next lesson. Or the bit of the park where the older children hang out, that you have to pass on your way home.

So – you know what is bullying and not 'just teasing'. And you know you have to stop and think what positive things you want to happen in the end. You have your positive 'self-motto' ready ("I am friendly, brave and brilliant at football!") and you've thought of a great 'other-motto' for the main bully ("I may not like him, but he is strong, clever and a great goal scorer"). You might still feel your heart sink with fright as you are about to walk past him in the corridor. Suppose you can see he and his mates are just waiting for someone to pick on? When they say, "Hello, little boy…" in menacing tones, instead of trying to disappear into the wall, what about distracting them by saying something to them that they would *like*, such as, "Great goal last night!"

Again you are going to need to practise this one...

Get your mum or dad or a friend to pretend to be the bully.

Either they can walk up to you looking nasty, or you can walk up to them as they give you bad looks! (This is so brilliant – not only are you going to be good at stopping bullying by the end of this book, you are going to be great at acting too!)

Anyway, in this exercise however they look or whatever they say it will be YOUR task to say something nice that makes them feel good about themselves – and that will stop them putting you down.

This next exercise is a bit sneaky but give it a try...

Next time you leave your bedroom in a complete mess, or you've done something you know is wrong, use this strategy with your mum. As she comes up the stairs in a huge rage to get you... *go towards her and say something nice about one of the things she does for you* (this is easy because she does loads of nice things for you).

What happened? Were you surprised that just saying nice (but true) things to people could make them stop being horrible to you? Excellent, that's ANOTHER successful strategy under your belt!

By the way, I am a mum too and I have to tell you that you may have stopped me being so *cross* with you but *you still need to tidy up your room! NOW!*

Reward (Because you deserve it!)

I left this strategy to the very end and it might look as if I'm going to say, "Because you have done so well, you now deserve a treat!" Not so! I think that just because you are TRYING to sort out bullying in such a positive way you deserve a treat.

What kind of treat? Well, since we're dealing in positive things in this book, what about positive treats? Not things that cost money because not everyone can afford that. You know the sort of things you can do without money – kick a ball around with your mates, read a really good book, stroke the cat or dog, giggle with your friends, splash around in mud... Just add things you like doing that make you feel good without harming you or anyone else!

Stopping yourself from doing the same things you've always done when you're worried or upset is a big task. It can feel as if you're trying to be a whole different person and that's exhausting. Of course, you're *not* trying to do that. You're only trying to be the best version of you that you can manage each day. Some days it's easy, other days it's... a NIGHTMARE! But the point is you are trying. In trying to sort out bullying in positive ways that make everyone else feel better as well as you, you are, in fact, making the world a nicer place for the rest of us to live in. Thank you.

So rewarding yourself for trying to do this on the days you get it right AND the days you get it wrong is an excellent strategy. It reminds you that you are trying. And it shows the rest of us that you are a worthwhile person who deserves to be treated with respect.

The TEN strategies...

1. BULLYING ?

You know that if you feel bullied you're right – even if the person didn't mean to bully you. And you know you have to do something about it fast to make yourself feel better!

2. STOP&THINK!

You also know that you have to be sure what you want to happen in the end because if you want other kids / teachers / parents to like you, you need to be extra careful about what you do to sort stuff out.

3. SELF-MOTTO

Remember! Most kids bully because they have found that each time they put someone else down, they feel a bit better about themselves. When they feel low, they start looking for that person who  looks easy to put down. *Now* you know that if you *feel* sad and frightened, you probably *look* sad and frightened. So you will quickly realise that the bully will see you as one of those easy targets! They put you down... and feel better. And you feel even worse. So get a store of strong, positive self-mottos ready, fast!

4. OTHER-MOTTO

You also have to remember that bullies don't just pick up on how you feel about *yourself*, they pick up on how you feel about *them* too! You NEED to remember the 1... 2... 3... good points about others as well as the bad points so that it's that much easier to sort things out and be the popular kind of person that you deserve to be!

5. DISTRACTION

This means that although you can't ignore the actual bully (because they need your attention so badly they are prepared to be nasty in order to get it), you can choose to ignore what they actually said or did because you can't deal with that right now. The trick here is to distract them from what they said by talking about something completely different.

6. HUMOUR

Judging what other people find funny is a risky thing! They *might* think you are very, very witty and want to be your friend forever. Or they might think you are being sarcastic and rude! Being able to tell a joke against yourself every now and then is fine. Just don't do it too often – the important thing is for you to feel good about yourself and your ability to handle bullies, not put yourself down all the time.

7. FRIENDS

Not only are you less likely to be picked on when you're with friends, you will also have people to talk through any bullying that's happened and how you want to sort it out. Learning to make friends is a skill you can learn like any other skill. You find out how to do it and you practise and practise and practise until you can do it!

8. APPEARANCE

How you look matters. If you look as if you have taken care over your appearance others will notice that. And they will also notice if you haven't taken care. And then they will make decisions about you based on that. It's not about designer labels, it's about looking as if you treat yourself with respect.

9. FLATTERY

People who bully feel insecure in some way. Giving them a genuine compliment gives them positive attention so that they feel better about themselves.

10. REWARD

Sorting out bullying is very satisfying when you get it right. It's also jolly tiring. So give yourself the kind of positive treats that give you a bit more energy (like enough sleep and good food). And remind yourself, when you enjoy those rewards, that you're one of those important people in this world who tries to help things to get better, not worse.

ADULTS – CHAPTER 6

USING ALL THE STRATEGIES!

Finally sorting it out:

In the past I've been good to you. I've trawled through my life and exposed my failures to you like there's no tomorrow! Now it's your turn! I really need you to have a go at this! I have total faith in you...

Strategy 1: Bullying?

Think of a situation in which you yourself have felt humiliated. Was it *really* bullying? Or just a bit of teasing? Are you being hypersensitive here? No? You stick by what you said – you felt bullied? Fantastic! Now you don't need to waste any more precious energy wondering if you're also a failure because you don't even know what is or is not bullying. You *were* bullied and now you want to sort it out.

I now need you to write out what happened. It doesn't matter whether it is to do with your child and bullying, or something entirely different that you find distressing. Just write it out in all its overwhelming horridness.

Savour, for the very last time, feeling hopeless about this. And then get on with the exercises below and show yourself who's in charge now!

Strategy 2: Stop & Think!

You've now said what it was that upset you so much. You are entitled to feel upset and angry. But after a little while (how long will depend on just how serious the bullying was) you need to stop and think about what you would like to happen so that you can put this upset and anger behind you. If all you want is to get even (revenge), there's not much I can do to help you yet. But as soon as you decide that you want to end up feeling genuinely good about yourself *and* your ability to sort things out so that everyone behaves that much better... read on!

Strategy 3: Self-motto

No matter how awful it is, due to the horridness of the situation in which you find yourself, write down your 'self-motto' *at your most wretched*:

I feel...

How does this terrible, upset, angry feeling affect your facial expression, your body language, and the way you behave?

My facial expression is...

My body language (e.g. eye contact / shoulders / hands)...

How I probably behave...

Now describe how you think the negative way you look and behave might affect the person who is distressing you.

They will probably...

And how does the way they treat you (based on your silent, negative self-motto) make you feel now? Better about yourself? Or actually even worse about yourself?

I feel...

If, like most of us, your first reaction to a bad situation was to feel anxious and upset by the whole thing, at least you now understand that this affects how you look and behave. Not only does a negative self-motto increase your own feeling of helplessness, the subtle, weak messages you give out are picked up by others (because their brains are programmed to do so). Some of those other people will assume that if you do not feel good about yourself, you do not deserve respect. This will make you feel even worse about yourself.

The solution is clear. You need to change those subtle messages in order to change others' reactions. For the sake of your self-esteem, you need to end up feeling better, not worse about yourself.

Time to put on a CD of 'I will survive', or 'Born to be wild', boogie around for a bit, punch your fist in the air and then give yourself a good, powerful self-motto that will give you mental confidence to deal with that bully! Name THREE of your best qualities.

I am also...

Describe how this positive, powerful self-motto affects your facial expression now. What about your body language? And your behaviour?

My facial expression now is...

My body language now shows (eye contact / shoulders / hands)...

My behaviour now...

How is the bully likely to react to you *now*?

And now that you feel good about yourself, and the bully is reacting to your new subtle messages, do you still feel bad, or is there a light beginning to dawn on this situation, as you feel better about yourself? WELL DONE! Hold on to this self-motto when faced with this particular bully.

In other situations, and with other bullying behaviours, you may need to have other positive self-mottos. You might like to make a note of these. Eventually you will end up with lots that you can call up at will whenever you feel low about something or some one!

The vital thing to remember here is that a strong self-motto will result in confident body language. Not only will this increase your feeling of being in control of yourself, the subtle, strong messages you give out are picked up by others. Some of these other people will assume that if you feel good about yourself, you deserve respect. They will treat you positively. If you want to feel good about yourself, this will make you feel even better!

Strategy 4: Other-motto

We've already dealt with the way you feel about the child who bullies yours in an earlier chapter. What I'd like you to do here is to think about the way you feel about your *own* child and see how that influences the way you help them deal with bullying.

When your child comes home from school looking wretched and defeated from another day of teasing and bullying, what is your other-motto about your child?

I feel they are...

How does the way you feel about them affect your facial expressions?

What about your body language?

How do you behave towards them?

Now tell me what messages you are giving your child about their ability to cope with bullying.

Will this make them feel better, or worse about themselves?

If you were like most of us, your initial reaction to this woe-begotten little mite will probably go one of two ways. You may want to comfort them and reassure them that you will defend them to the death.

Or you may feel irritable that they have got picked on yet again. Either way your other-motto is sending out clear messages in your facial expressions, body language and behaviour. This not only increases your feelings of helplessness / irritation *it increases their feelings of helplessness or irritation too!*

Try changing the way you feel to see if this helps. Think about them as strong, positive young people who are learning to deal with a difficult world. Make assumptions about their ability to cope and come out of this experience as stronger and wiser. Give them a new, positive 'other-motto'!

My child is also...

How does this new, positive other-motto affect *your* facial expressions?

What about your body language?

And your behaviour?

Does you feeling positive about your child help them to see that you are confident about their strengths? That however much someone else puts them down, you are right behind them in picking themselves up again? And how will this powerful support make your child feel about themselves?

My child will probably now feel...

Young children gain the bulk of their self-esteem from their parents. If parents think well of their children, those children have higher self-esteem. And if children have higher self-esteem they are more able to cope with bad things that come their way as they grow up. Neat, isn't it?

Strategy 5: Distraction

What would you do if you were standing at the bus stop with your child and the elderly lady in front started to tell you about her sad life? You might, in the spirit of showing your child the importance of being understanding and friendly, listen sympathetically as they describe the awfulness of living alone in a bedsit. However, as they feel encouraged by your interest, suppose they now launch into details of a lurid sex life? Your child looks up at you to see how you will react!

What did you decide as your child watched you for clues on how to behave? It would be impossible to *actually* ignore this rant as you are stuck in the queue waiting for that bus! And you are probably unlikely to think it is OK to verbally abuse someone so elderly, however foul-mouthed they have turned out to be! The likelihood is that you frantically thought up ways to distract her from her tirade! I bet you said firmly something along the lines of, "Isn't it freezing? Is it me, or has it got colder the last few days?"

Bad behaviour can't always be ignored, but does that justify *us* behaving badly? Unless you are determined to follow this old lady home and contact social services, distracting people behaving inappropriately by changing the subject and leading them on to something neutral is a brilliant life skill. Having your child watch you practise this successfully is just the icing on the cake.

And the thing *you* felt bullied by? How could *you* have used the Distraction strategy to defuse the difficult situation you were in?

I could have…

Strategy 6: Humour

You are racing through the housework on your day off. The doorbell goes. Grabbing armfuls of dirty laundry from the bathroom floor ("Why, oh why, is there always so much of the stuff?"), you race downstairs. The nosy neighbour from down the road stands there on your doorstep. To explain your somewhat dishevelled appearance you say, "I'm just about to do all the laundry! She responds, smugly, "I just have to be organised. I do mine every day!" How do you react to this? Smother her in dirty laundry? Imply that you have better things to do with your time than keep up with washing? Give her a big grin and salute her as an obviously superior being?

All these responses could be, in their own way, funny. But if you want to defuse the situation (rather than win at all costs and risk her telling the rest of the street that you have *absolutely no sense of humour!*) probably the third solution, where you are able to laugh at yourself, will always be the best one!

I don't know, of course, what *you* felt bullied by and whether being able to make a joke was appropriate. Or whether a wry smile at yourself was all that was needed. Only you know the answer to that.

Strategy 7: Friends

Those of us who can name about four or five good friends tend to feel better and have better mental health than those who can only name one. It's partly a gambling odds thing – if one friendship goes wrong, you've still got enough people left to not feel totally abandoned!

But how can you tell if they *are* good friends when it comes to you feeling bullied about something? Apart from shared interests or a similar sense of humour, a good friend will understand when you say you are upset and angry because someone has distressed you. A good friend will not add to that distress by saying you're being too sensitive and get over it. And even though together you may laugh about a response that would involve revenge, in the long run a good friend will help you towards a solution that empowers everyone – including you.

Make a list! Which friends do you have who are genuinely supportive of you? Who else do you know that you would like to become friendly with to add to your list?

Let your children know why you value these good friends.

Strategy 8: Appearance

Most of us know that what we wear affects how others react to us. The Queen wears relatively conservative clothes partly because she does not want to offend peoples' ideas on how a Queen *should* dress. A rock and roll star will dress to be noticed. People wear uniforms so that we can make quick assessments of what it is they do and whether they could be useful or threatening to us. And the same goes for you too when trying to fit in socially with a group. You will tend to adopt a similar 'uniform' of clothes. Of course, you may be unable, for religious or cultural reasons, to do this. If so you will have to work *particularly* hard on all the other strategies so that you are not seen as a threat just because you look different from them!

In considering your personal situation of being bullied, please bear the following in mind. *Whatever you decide to wear, however you decide to look – make sure it helps you to feel confident.* Worrying about the way you look when trying to tackle a bullying situation is distracting. Look the absolute best of what you want to be. And then ignore your appearance and concentrate on using the rest of the strategies. This way you can change this situation from one where you feel bad about yourself into one where you feel a whole lot better about yourself!

Strategy 9: Flattery

Some people find giving compliments really easy. Others find it really hard. Which one are you? One of the powerful things about being confident about *ourselves* is that this confidence makes it easier to empower others by giving them compliments.

Imagine this: sunny day, new shoes, good journey into work, feeling great! You breeze into the office and see the nervous new secretary in her / his new suit. It is so easy to be generous and say, "Love the new suit!" But what about the day that it pours with rain and you have now ruined your new shoes? Is it still as easy to make that compliment? Probably not!

So what about your case, where you have described someone bullying you? Could you give them a compliment *even though you understand now that the bully has wobbly self-esteem and needs to put you down in order to feel better about themselves?* Armed with that positive other-motto you came up with about them a few pages back, try a *genuine* compliment and watch their reaction! Chances are they'll first look startled and then pleased. And then watch them as they mentally reassess you as the much-nicer-than-they-had-thought person that you actually are.

Strategy 10: Reward

Working successfully through bullying issues is not only immensely satisfying, it is also *exhausting!* Having a strong self-motto and maintaining it in the face of aggression is like being an actor stuck in a 24-

hour play! However successful the actor is, however much everyone applauds and stamps and cheers – that actor will still feel shattered by the end! Your task here is to find some kind of positive reward for yourself that doesn't involve over-indulging in anything that will make you – or anyone else for that matter – feel worse! It means finding the kind of reward that will give you MORE energy... I'm going to say this even though I sound like the very old, boring granny I undoubtedly am... Nuts, seeds, herbal tea and a good night's sleep are always going to help you feel more able to tackle anything life will throw at you tomorrow than are chocolate cake and whisky. Well maybe just a *small* slice and a thimbleful wouldn't hurt! But then do the herbal tea and bed sketch as well!

And finally:

The purpose of this book was to give you and your family choices about how you deal with aggressive people and situations. Do you remember in the first chapter when I told you what kids themselves had said about bullying? I'd like to have one more look at it with you to check that we've covered all the angles!

- *What kids particularly wanted was a range of skills that would give them choices in how to deal positively with awkward situations.* Well, we've definitely covered that one! Just having a fantastic self-motto or being good at cracking jokes *is not enough.* To get the very most out of life (and not feel unduly threatened by *anyone*) we all need a whole range of positive strategies.

- *Kids don't just want bullying to stop, they also want to be liked by other kids – even by the bullies (who are sometimes their friends).* We covered this in the Stop&Think! strategy. Isolation is a very scary position indeed. Every time there is bullying we now know to check very carefully what outcome our child wants.

- *Kids want to know how to sort out minor bullying for themselves rather than having to rely on adults.* No problem! You now have TEN ways of empowering them to do this! The fact that you trust them to have a go is also immensely empowering for them.

- *The ways of coping that kids use most are hitting and shouting back or running away and truanting.* Running away when you are *physically* threatened is a very smart move indeed and one I would always advise. But by working through this book with them you have given them TEN positive options to sort out *psychological* bullying in positive ways.

- *Kids also say that when they ask adults what else they could do, they are told to either ignore bullies or tell an adult.* A result I hadn't expected when I started this work was that once kids had a range of positive strategies that built up their self-belief they suddenly *were* able to ignore the minor bullying that goes on. Just as importantly, they now knew when it was time to *either* be assertive (and say NO!

very firmly) or call in an adult to help. This is very important indeed because it means that *if we give our children the tools they need to sort out psychological bullying they will be better equipped to deal with physical bullying.*

As well as all the ones I've shared with you, there will be other very successful strategies that you know about. If these strategies are positive – and respectful of others as well as yourself – I would be very honoured if you would add them to this list.

You are an absolutely star parent to work through all this in order to help your child. Good luck and all my very, very best wishes.

Kids – Chapter 6

Right! Even though it's been pretty hard work, we've now had a go at using TEN positive strategies. So far I think we've done really well, don't you? But if you're like most people, you will have found some of the exercises easier to do than others. What you *might* now be thinking is that you'll just do the strategies that you found easy. *Please, please don't think this!* Why not? Because, however hard you find some of them, *the*

more strategies you can use well, the better you will feel about being able to stop bullying. To prove my point, I want you to read this story and tell me how YOU would use ALL the strategies to sort out the bullying that's happening to *somebody else...*

When Gemma was ten years old she was in a bad car accident. Gemma's dad was driving. Gemma's mum was sat in the front seat beside him. Gemma's baby brother was in his special car seat, in the back with her. As they came round a sharp corner, another car was coming fast towards them, on the wrong side of the road. It crashed into their car. Gemma's mum was killed. Her dad and her baby brother were unhurt. Gemma's window was smashed and a lot of the glass cut her face. She has had to go into hospital several times for really painful operations to repair the damage from the glass, but afterwards she is still left with two big scars. One is across one of her eyes and makes her face look uneven. The other one goes across her top lip, right up to her nose.

While all this was happening, Gemma was at junior school. All her friends had known her since she was little and they were all really kind to her. They didn't care about the two bad scars because Gemma was their friend.

Now Gemma is eleven and has just started secondary school. Her dad has decided to move house because the old house reminds him too much of Gemma's mum (who he misses terribly). So Gemma now has to go to a school where nobody knows her.

Some of the kids at the new school give her a really hard time laughing at her scars and making nasty remarks about the way that Gemma looks. She is very upset and miserable and wants to leave but her dad says she has to get on with it, these kids are just ignorant and teasing her...

I need you to imagine that you are Gemma's friend. Would you now be able to use ALL the strategies to help her? Have a go!

Strategy 1: BULLYING?
Question – Do YOU think Gemma was being bullied?

The teacher and her dad say, "Nobody has hit her. They're only being normal kids and she has to learn to live with it!" Do you think this is right? No, and nor do I. Bullying doesn't have to be about being hit. It is also when others say mean and nasty things either to you, or behind your back. Gemma is right to feel bullied and you are right to want to help her. *You* know that if you feel bullied you have been – even if others say it was 'only' teasing. So is Gemma now going to feel angry and upset?

What do YOU think her self-motto might be at the moment?

Write in what you think SHE might say:

I am...

If Gemma feels like this, what do you think her face will show (might she look sad or angry or frightened)?

What about her body language (things like does she look these kids in the eye, and is she all hunched up)?

How does she behave (does she cry, or keep fussing the teacher, or be badly behaved herself)?

How do you think her behaving this way affects the way that the bullies treat her?

Do you think that the way the bullies treat her (based on those secret messages she gives out about herself) makes her feel better, or worse about herself?

She will feel...

Of course, I'm guessing here, but did you think (from the story) that she felt ugly and lonely? And that because she felt this she kept away from other kids and didn't look them in the eye or try to be friendly? Do you think that now everyone (not just the bullies) might think that she was a bit stuck-up (and forget they'd been mean to her)? Or that she didn't like any of them? If they DID think anything like this, I guess they would *all* stop even thinking about being friendly, don't you? And now she would feel much worse about herself.

Strategy 2 – Stop&Think!

You have learnt that before you can do ANYTHING you have to be sure what you want to happen in the end. What does Gemma want to happen?

She wants...

Who put that she wants to make friends? TEN gold stars to you! As you know, if you want other kids / teachers / parents to like you, you need to be extra careful about what you do to sort stuff out. Gemma desperately wants to have friends at her new school so that means she can't do any of the shouting back / running away kinds of strategies that she might want to do...

Strategy 3 – Self-Motto

You've told us what you think Gemma's self-motto probably is when she feels powerless. But you and I know that because she feels sad and frightened, she probably looks sad and frightened, so the bullies think she's an easy target! Gemma needs to get a store of strong, positive self-mottos ready, fast!

So if Gemma came to YOU for advice, what kind of self-motto might you advise her to have? After all, you know some things about her. Like she has had to be very brave and she will have had to do lots of looking after her baby brother, and help her dad. Help Gemma find a new, positive self-motto!

I am...

How does this new, positive self-motto affect her facial expressions?

She looks...

What about her new, positive body language?

She will...

Last of all, how might she behave towards other kids now that she feels so much better about herself?

She might...

And does she feel better about herself? I think we know the answer to that one! Because you have helped her change her self-motto to something *positive*, you have helped her change the way she looks and the way she behaves. You have made her feel much better. Well done!

When others are mean to us, it isn't surprising if we feel mean back! You also have to remember that bullies don't just pick up on how Gemma feels about *herself*, they pick up on how she feels  about *them* too! You NEED to remember the 1... 2... 3... good points about others as well as the bad points so that it's that much easier to sort things out and be the popular kind of person that you deserve to be!

The trouble is, if Gemma doesn't know this, when she's being bullied, what do YOU think she might think about those bullies who make fun of her after she has lost her mum and been in a terrible accident?

Write in what you think she would say:

They are...

If Gemma feels like this, what do you think her face will show (might she look sad or angry or frightened)?

Her face will look...

What about her body language (things like does she look these kids in the eye, is she all hunched up, or are her fists clenched up, ready for a fight)?

How does she behave (does she cry, or keep

fussing the teacher, or is she now badly behaved herself)?

How do you think her behaving this way affects the way that the bullies treat her?

They…

Do you think that the way they will now treat her (based on her other-motto for the bullies) makes her feel better, or worse about herself?

She feels…

So, watching how Gemma behaves when she hates these other kids, can you see that even though they were the nasty ones in the first place, they now tell others that it's OK to be nasty to her because she is nasty back to them? So because her secret feelings about the bullies show in the way she looks and in her behaviour, she ends up feeling even worse about herself.

So if Gemma came to YOU for advice again, what kind of other-motto might you get her to have? I'm trusting you to find her a new, positive other-motto to change things around (remember it has to be something that Gemma respects – like the bullies are also good with little kids, and they raise money for charity). If you get stuck for positive words, look back at the list in Chapters 2 and 3!

They are also…

How does this new, positive other-motto affect the way her face looks?

She looks…

What about her new, positive body language?

She…

Last of all, how might she behave towards other kids now that she feels so much better about them?

She might…

What a star you are! I wish you were MY friend! You gave her a strong, positive other-motto and this meant that she could see that the bullies weren't all bad. This helped her to be a bit friendlier herself and that stopped other kids thinking she was stuck-up. Because of your helpful other-motto she now feels much better about herself.

Strategy 5 – Distraction

This means that although Gemma can't ignore the actual bullies (because they need her attention so badly they are prepared to be nasty in order to get it), she can choose to ignore what they actually said or did because she can't deal with that right now. The trick here is to distract those bullies somehow…

Even if we get Gemma to change her self-motto and her other-motto, some kids might *still* not get the message and say the odd horrid thing. As you know, it's not easy to just ignore them (because the bullies want her to react to them!) and the teacher will not be happy if she screams bad things back at them. What could Gemma say that would ignore their stupid remarks but still give them attention so that they stop being rude to her?

Another TEN gold stars if you thought of saying something like, "Do you know where the homework timetables are?" It just changes the topic!

Strategy 6 – Humour

Am I serious? Do I want you to find something funny for this girl who has had a horrible accident, lost her mum, changed schools and because of this lost all her old friends too? How can I possibly suggest that she make funny remarks? Well I do suggest that. Which remark do you think will be the best one to win friends when the bullies call her 'scary face'?

1. "Takes one to know one!"
2. "This is my special face for geography lessons! I'm hoping to frighten the teacher into not giving us any homework!"

I hope that you said the last one because it's the one where SHE WAS ABLE TO LAUGH AT HERSELF and this is the one *most* likely to get the others to think she's at least got a good sense of humour.

But please remember that judging what other people find funny is a risky thing! They *might* think Gemma is being really funny and want to be her friend forever. Or they might think she was being sarcastic and rude!

And also remember that being able to tell a joke against herself every now and then is fine. But she shouldn't do it too often – the important thing is for her to feel good about herself and her ability to handle bullies, not put herself down all the time.

Strategy 7 – Friends

What if Gemma said that she didn't need friends at school because she had her old friends that she talked to on her mobile? Do you think this would be OK? No! Nor do I! We need to have friends around us because it's safer that way. If she stays on her own she is MUCH more likely to get picked on. So I hope you would get her to make some new friends! If she came to YOUR school she would already have you, and that's a brilliant start. You could also explain to her that learning to make new friends is just a skill you can learn. You just need to practise and practise and practise until you can do it!

Strategy 8 – Appearance

Now, you already understand that

bullies feel better about themselves if they put some other kid down. The easiest person to do this to is the kid who is a lot different from most of you. It could be the kid who dresses very differently. Or the kid who talks differently. What about the kid whose mum or dad doesn't wash their kids' clothes often enough? What if, like Gemma, it was because you looked different because you had been ill, or in an accident, or you were just born that way?

The point about the way that we look is this: we should be confident about it. You might feel confident wearing bright pink or blue shorts. So that's good. But I would feel awful in those shorts because I like wearing long black trousers! So that's what I wear and I feel good too. We only have a problem if you say I've GOT to wear pink shorts even though I hate them on me! Gemma has a problem because she hates her scars. How do you think you could help her to feel better about them? What would help you if you were Gemma?

There is no answer I can give you for this. We're all different. How YOU cope might be more useful to Gemma than how I would cope because at least you're around the same age so more likely to understand how best to fit in. I can back off a bit on this one because I'm confident that your advice would be good.

There are still TWENTY gold stars out there for those of you who said that you now think that the way she looks is no longer so important. That Gemma could get away with pretty much *anything* as long as she has a really strong, positive self-motto!

Strategy 9 – Flattery (saying something nice)

Would YOU want to say something nice to a kid who was mean to you? I don't expect Gemma wants to either. But it's another great way of distracting somebody (making them think of something else). It's also a great way of helping somebody to like you! After all, most of us like to feel that we're popular. And if you're popular, bullies are *much* less likely to pick on you.

What sort of compliment (nice thing) could Gemma to say to the bullies (perhaps something nice about their hair or the fact that they raise money for charity)? The important thing is that she means it – because bullies can spot a fake really easily! Giving them a genuine compliment gives them positive attention so that they feel better about themselves – and that means that Gemma is MORE likely to get what she wants – friends.

Strategy 10 – Reward

Last of all, I want you to remember what I said about bullying. Do you remember that I said it was about using energy to get power? If Gemma is serious about sorting out bullying, she, just like you, has to work up some energy. Not only that, I hope that you can also see that Gemma stands a much better chance of sorting all this bullying out if she tries using ALL the strategies. Just having a good self-motto or having friends isn't enough. Sometimes the most important thing is being able to joke, sometimes even her new friends won't be around her. What would she do then without all the back-ups? Your job is to get her to understand that she needs all of them to be really successful.

So she also needs to decide what sort of treats, or rewards she wants to give herself for sorting out the bullying for herself (with your help obviously)! If she's using up lots of extra energy she might decide to give herself the kind of treats that will give her that boost! It's a bit boring but getting enough sleep, eating good food and drinking lots of water will actually help! She AND you need to give yourselves those positive treats to build up the extra energy you need and to remind you both that you're actually very important people in this world because you try to help things get better, not worse.

Last of all:

By the end of this book I had always hoped that you would be able to start sorting out the kind of bullying where kids say mean things or leave you out of stuff. But now I'm hoping that you will not only be able to stop other kids bullying you – but you will be able to stop them bullying others too! Bit of a tall order, but you have come through so much in this book. I think that you can do it. Best of all, I think that now, at long last, YOU think that way too. Your parents will be very proud of you. Your teachers will be very proud of you. And I am *extremely* proud of you!